THE X FACTOR

THE X FACTOR

A QUEST FOR EXCELLENCE

George Plimpton

W. W. NORTON & COMPANY

NEW YORK/LONDON

Copyright © 1995, 1990 by George Plimpton

First published as a Norton paperback 1996

Excerpt from *Barbarians at the Gate: The Fall of RJR Nabisco*
by Bryan Burrough and John Helyar. Copyright © 1990 by
Bryan Burrough and John Helyar. Reprinted by permission
of HarperCollins Publishers, Inc.

The text of this book is composed in Sabon with the display set in Poster Bodini
and Arcadia. Composition and manufacturing by the Haddon Craftsmen, Inc.
Book design by JoAnne Metsch.

Library of Congress Cataloging-in-Publication Data

Plimpton, George.
The X Factor : a quest for excellence / George Plimpton.
p.   cm.
1. Achievement motivation. 2. Excellence—Psychological aspects.
3. Performance. 4. Success—Psychological aspects. 5. Bush, George, 1924- .
I. Title
BF503.P48   1995
158'.1—dc20   94-27933
ISBN 0-393-31468-5

W.W. Norton & Company, Inc., 500 Fifth Avenue, New York, N.Y. 10110
W.W. Norton & Company Ltd., 10 Coptic Street, London WC1A 1PU

3 4 5 6 7 8 9 0

For T.P., Susie, Peter, and Jane

Introduction

A FEW YEARS AGO, Whittle Communications L.P. asked me to do a short work on a "subject of importance to managers and policymakers in business and the public sector." I brooded about this for a while, wondering if they'd picked the right man for the job, and then concluded it might be interesting to write an informal study of the ingredient that appears to be a constant for those who are enormously successful. The "X Factor" I called it, though it is a quality which goes by many aliases: competitive spirit, the will to win, giving it 110 percent, the hidden spark, Celtic Green, Yankee pinstripes (once upon a time), guts, the killer instinct, élan vital, having the bit in one's teeth, and so on—qualities which if synthesized into a liquid form and corked up in a bottle could be sold by the millions.

The Whittle people allowed me to go ahead. They asked me to interview a few highly successful people in the world of business. In turn, since my own field has included sports, I called on a number of topflight athletes and coaches to see what they had to say about the X Factor. Whether a comparison can be made between business and sports is problematic. Sports, after all, has often been described as a microcosm of life, though it should be remembered that it doesn't tell you very much about being in debt, or love, or marriage, or bringing up children. But then perhaps the world of business doesn't either.

The framework of *The X Factor*—the bookends, if you will—is made up of descriptions of a pair of horseshoe matches I played with George Bush while on assignment from *Sports Illustrated*. The first of these matches was not long after his election to the presidency in 1989, and the second in the spring of the following year. Indeed, it was the dire result of the first match that inspired me to look into the X Factor ingredient which lurks somewhere in the systems of certain fortunates, certainly Bush, and allows them to outdo themselves whether in sports, business, or politics.

Whittle Communications L.P. sent what was put together of all this—a thin, near-quarto-sized book (with advertising pages from Federal Express)—to a selected list of CEOs around the country.

More recently, W. W. Norton, the publishing house, decided to bring out *The X Factor* in a more traditional way. To my delight, its editors have given me the opportunity to add some new material. Bush was, of course, defeated in the 1992 election, perhaps diminishing him as an avatar of the X Factor, though it should be remembered that even such a competitive spirit as his does not necessarily guarantee success, especially in a science as puzzling and uncertain as politics. He was nice enough to see me yet a third time, and our conversation appears as a kind of coda at the end of the book.

One of the impulses in doing this sort of research was that some of the X Factor ingredients might rub off on me, as well as on the reader, and that a careful reading of the text and perhaps the practice of one or two of the exercises described could result in a mild transformation. One's habitual nemesis (at least mine) in the second round of the country-club tournament—the elderly man with the hearing aid and the steady forehand—will no longer be a stumbling block. I cannot promise as much, since it hasn't happened in my case. But one can hope for the best.

THE X FACTOR

1

THINK IT WAS a Wednesday, the first day of the working
week at *Sports Illustrated*. The managing editor called me
into his office.

"Bush," he said.

As he paused, leaning back in his chair, I thought he
was referring to a small piece I had written a few weeks
before.

"The president," he said. "Do you know him?"

"No."

"Well, we're doing him. Photographs. History. Yale,
all that stuff, and we'd like you to go down and see him."

I nodded.

As he began describing George Bush's athletic background, a *Sports Illustrated* profile seemed an obvious
choice since the president was an avid fisherman and bird
shot, a member of championship soccer and baseball
teams in his undergraduate days at Yale, a wrestler in the

navy, a fine squash, tennis, and golf player, and, most recently—as we all had read in the press—an enthusiast at horseshoes.

"A wrestler in the navy?"

"That's what the clips say," the managing editor said. He suggested I spend some time in the magazine's library . . . not only checking into the George Bush file, but boning up on the athletic backgrounds of other presidents to compare. "Teddy Roosevelt," he said. "Shot a lot of animals. I believe Nixon was a bowler."

I spent a couple of days doing this. Some presidents had no interest in sports at all. Thomas Jefferson once remarked, "Games played with the ball are too violent for the body and stamp no character on the mind." Abraham Lincoln, on the other hand, was described as "hard as nails, a good horseman, swimmer, crowbar heaver, and master jumper." He reportedly could hold a heavy ax out at arm's length for an astonishing length of time, which he occasionally did as a kind of parlor trick. Teddy Roosevelt played tennis during his White House tenure. The *Sports Illustrated* library had a photograph of him wearing an old pair of trousers and holding the racket halfway up the shaft. Herbert Hoover, the least athletic-looking president except perhaps for the 300-pound Howard Taft, played a medicine-ball game invented by the White House physician for him to lose weight. A photograph showed a group of bulky men in suits, Hoover among them, standing on the White House lawn staring at a medicine ball as if it had dropped heavily and mysteriously among them from the sky. Harry Truman, who was ambidextrous, pitched horseshoes left-handed on the White House lawn and threw out Opening Day baseballs right-handed one year, left-handed the next—with the puzzling explanation that he was doing it for the benefit of the photographers.

Richard Nixon—just as the managing editor suspected—often went down to the bowling lanes in the basement of the Executive Office Building, very often playing alone, bowling in shirt and tie, watched by a small coterie of Secret Service men. On one occasion, presumably to get his mind off his troubles, he bowled twenty games in a row. The best game of his career was listed as a remarkable 232. In the files, a photograph snapped just as he let the ball go shows him with his front foot half over the fault line.

A host of presidential golfers turned up in the research—Woodrow Wilson, who waved off a messenger bringing him the news that he had secured the Democratic nomination until he could sink a putt; Warren Harding, who trained his dog, Laddie Boy, to shag balls for him on the White House lawn; Dwight Eisenhower, who played daily while at the Summer White House at Newport, Rhode Island, with the Secret Service disguised rather halfheartedly as caddies, their clubs in canvas golf bags clinking against the stocks of their carbines as they moved down the fairways.

The most noted golfer was undoubtedly Gerald Ford, whose rounds were distinguished by errant shots, which more than once conked a spectator. Bob Hope—as I read in the files—once remarked that his partners in a favorite foursome would be Gerald Ford, a faith-healer, and a paramedic!

The file on George Bush contained clippings and a packet of photographs. One of the latter showed him in the baggy baseball uniform of his Andover prep-school days. Hands on hips, a slight smile, he was identified as

Poppy Bush, and the caption read "Watch out, Exeter, we're going to win." Another showed him at Yale, again in a baseball outfit, standing next to Babe Ruth during an onfield award ceremony. A few of the more contemporary shots were of him on a tennis court with Bjorn Borg as a doubles partner, another tossing up a hook shot in a family backyard basketball game. One of the players in the game was wearing a T-shirt with the slogan *Dukakis Don't Mess with Texas*. There were a few of Bush fishing, and one in hunting gear, perhaps in Texas quail country.

I closed the file and walked down the corridor to see the managing editor.

"I don't know what to expect," I said.

He shrugged. He said the magazine was sending a photographer down to Florida where Bush was going on a pre-inauguration vacation. He smiled. "Maybe he'll get a photo of him down on the beach out bait-casting in some big surf. Real big surf," he added.

"You voted Democrat?"

He shrugged again. "I'm tired," he said. "Maybe the guy exhausts me."

■ ■ ■

I WENT DOWN to Washington just a week or so before the inauguration. We talked in the living room of the vice-president's official residence at the Naval Observatory. Mrs. Bush was with us, working on a needlepoint design of flowers. The atmosphere was very relaxed. The interview went well. Mr. Bush talked a lot about fishing—how it gave him time to relax from the rigors of work and to do some contemplative thinking. He quoted Izaak Walton's line about how the days a man spends fishing ought not to be deducted from his time on earth. He'd had only one long spell of government duty without fishing, and that was when he served as chief of the U.S. Liaison Office in Peking. Even there he'd had a chance. At a Soviet embassy party he was invited to sit in a boat at one end of a ceremonial pool, while at the other end an army of beaters got into the water and started driving a school of large carp toward him.

"Scary," Mr. Bush said. "Hundreds of these gigantic carp crashing around in the water. We waited for them with nets on the end of poles."

Barbara Bush remembered that what was caught was immediately cleaned by the Russian kitchen staff and prepared to take home. "The Russians had a beautiful complex built during the time of Peter the Great," she said. "They entertained a lot."

"Hockey games," the president-elect said. "On the lake. I was never much of a skater, so I didn't go out on the ice. I don't like to do things I can't do well. I don't dance well, so I don't dance.

"See this scar here?" he asked suddenly. He pointed to the back of his hand. A six-pound bluefish off Florida had nipped him. "Then I've got a scar here close to my eyebrow from a collision trying to head a ball playing soccer at Andover. Can't see it? Well, how about *this* one?" He pulled his shirt away from his neck to reveal a prominent bump on his right shoulder blade. "Got that one playing mixed doubles with Barbara at Kennebunkport. Ran into a porch."

"His mother always said that it was my shot," Barbara Bush said. "I didn't run for it, so he did. She was probably right."

The president-elect smiled and shrugged his shoulders. "Popped the shoulder out," he said. "Separated."

"After that, they moved the porch," his wife said with a smile.

Bush said that he had been playing tennis since he was about five. He had stopped playing singles not long after grade school and concentrated on doubles, largely because his ground strokes were "terrible," except for a backhand chip return of service that drops at the feet of the oncoming server and that he referred to as "the falling leaf."

A number of other home-grown phrases have developed in the Bush family over the years, and I was told what some of them were. A weak shot in tennis elicits the disdainful cry "power outage!" The most esoteric is "unleash Chiang!"—years ago an oft-used phrase during the hue and cry in government circles to allow Chiang Kai-shek to invade the Chinese mainland from Taiwan; on the Bush tennis court it refers to a potential source of power.

"George will look over his shoulder at his partner about to serve," Barbara Bush explained, "and urge him to *unleash Chiang!*"

"The interesting thing about these phrases," she went on, "is that they get exported; people take them with them, and off in the distance, from someone else's court, you'll suddenly hear, 'All right now, Jack, unleash Chiang!' "

"What are some others?" I asked.

I was informed that after serving up an ace in tennis or sinking a long putt on the golf course, Mr. Bush would often cry out, "Vic Damone!"

"The singer?" I looked puzzled.

The president-elect looked somewhat rueful. "It's what I say rather than 'victory.' I can't remember when I started doing it. A ringer will get it—a 'Vic Damone.' Hey," he said suddenly. "How about a game of horseshoes? You've done all these things. Football with the . . . "

"Detroit Lions."

"Right. And the Boston Bruins and all that. You gotta try some horseshoes."

I said I would be honored.

On the way through the house outside to the horseshoe court, Barbara Bush stopped me and said, "You'll have to wear a cowboy hat. No one with any self-respect plays horseshoes without a cowboy hat." She rummaged around in a closet just inside the front door. On a top shelf sat an assortment of Bush's hats. I tried on a few of the Western variety. His head is a lot larger than mine, so the hats tended to slide down my forehead nearly to my eyes.

"These hats all seem to be the same size," I remarked, a somewhat lunatic observation, since it implied that Mr. Bush wore hats of different head measurements.

I finally picked a tall-crowned model with the president-elect's name stamped in gold on the inside. I wore it out to the horseshoe pit at a curious raked angle, peering from under it so I could see where I was going. Mr. Bush stared briefly at it. His was decorated with a braided Indian cord that supplemented the hatband. He held out some horseshoes.

"You got a choice," he said. "The drop-forged eight or the ten."

"I'll take the . . . ah . . . "

The president-elect laughed. "I don't know the difference myself." He looked down at the horseshoes, lifting them to judge their weight. "They tell me the harder the metal, the more it tends to be rejected by the stake."

Then he explained the rules of the game: 1 point for the

shoe closest to the stake, 3 for the ringer, and the winner the first to reach 15 points. We took some practice throws. I threw my shoes so they revolved parallel to the ground toward the opposite stake. This somewhat startled Mr. Bush, since that is the style (though I was unaware) used by most topflight pitchers.

"Hey, what have we got here?" he asked suspiciously. He prefers to hold the shoe at its closed end and toss it so it turns once, ass over tea kettle, as it goes down the pitch.

"You played this game before?"

"Not for thirty years," I said truthfully.

The game began. Mr. Bush was supported loudly by his seven-year-old granddaughter, Jenna, who was seated at courtside bundled up in a bright orange parka. There was considerable chatter during play—needling and a plethora of the home-grown expressions: "power outage" for a halfhearted toss, "SDI" for a throw with a higher arc than usual, and "it's an ugly pit" for those times when no one's shoe was close to the stake. Once, when it was impossible to tell which of the two shoes had landed closer, the president-elect shouted, "The tool! Get the tool!"—a request echoed by those standing around watching.

The tool, which was fetched from the gardening shed, turned out to be an oversized navigator's dividers. The president-elect knelt in the pit and brushed the dirt away from the two horseshoes. He handled the gadget with great relish. In fact, all aspects of the game were carried on with considerable élan. On occasion, he turned to me and asked rhetorically, "Isn't this game great?" "Have you ever had a better time?" "Isn't this just great? Heaven!"

I *was* having a good time. The iron felt cool and comfortable to the grip. I peered out from under the brim of my hat and suddenly, after a number of one-pointers, threw a ringer. I found myself with 14 points and only one to go to win. Mr. Bush had 13. Cries of alarm rose from Jenna's chair.

I began to worry about winning. What would it do to the president-elect's confidence to lose to someone who hadn't thrown a horseshoe in thirty years? Would he brood? Would he have trouble with his inauguration speech? Suddenly slam the heel of his hand against his forehead at cabinet meetings? Stumble into the bushes at the Rose Garden? Talk out loud to himself at state dinners? Snap at Sununu?

I decided that I would credit my victory to the hat. "Beginner's luck," I was going to say. "This hat of yours, Mr. Bush! If it hadn't been for this cowboy hat . . . "

It seemed the perfect solution. Gracious. Self-effacing. Just the thing to say.

"Listen, we can't let this happen," the president-elect was saying as he stepped up to throw. He sighted down the pitch. As he swung his arm back, he produced another of his home-grown motivators; it wasn't "unleash Chiang." In this case it was "remember Iowa!" . . . called out in reference to his recovery from political adversity there (he lost to Bob Dole) during the election primaries. We watched the red horseshoe leave his hand, turn over once in flight, drop toward the pit with its prongs forward, and with a dreadful clang collect itself around the stake. A ringer! A total of 16 points and victory for the president-elect. He flung his arms straight up in triumph, a tremendous smile on his face. From her chair Jenna began yelping pleasantly.

I said as follows: "Nerts!"

I can't recall the last time I used that antique expression. Mr. Bush came toward me, his hand outstretched. "Isn't that great!" he said as I congratulated him. He wasn't talking about his win but the fact that the game had been so much fun. I agreed with him. 'Heaven!" he said.

We walked back to the residence. Up on the porch Barbara Bush suggested that we leave our shoes, muddy from the horseshoe pit, by the front door, so we wouldn't track mud on the carpets. I stepped out of my loafers. One of my socks had a hole in it. My big toe shone briefly until I pulled the sock forward. It dangled off the front of my foot and flopped as I followed the president-elect into the house. He wanted to give me a tour of the premises. I followed him upstairs, first to his closet-sized office with its photographs of the Cigarette boat *Fidelity*, which he takes out for bluefishing, and a mounted bonefish (TEN POUNDS EIGHT OUNCES read the plaque under it) with a little rubber shark riding its back, tossed up there by a grandchild.

We climbed the stairs to a dormitory-like room at the top of the house, where the older Bush children bunk out on the floor in sleeping bags when they come to visit. The nearest thing to a trophy case is up there—a shelf cluttered with the kind of shoe-box mementos one might find in the back of a teenager's closet: scuffed baseballs, one of them, I noted, signed by Joe DiMaggio with the inscription, "You make the office look great"; a football autographed by Roger Staubach, who wrote, "Thanks for giving a darn about friends"; a Keith Hernandez model first-baseman's mitt; a Chicago Cubs pennant; a 1988 Dodgers World Series baseball cap; an NASL soccer ball; two construction worker's hard hats; and a blood-red Arkansas Razorback novelty hat shaped like a boar's head.

The president-elect took the hat off the shelf and tried it on, the snout poking over his forehead.

"I'm not sure it suits you, sir," I said. "It would startle your constituency."

"Not in Arkansas," he said, putting it back.

He picked up one of the baseballs and began tossing it in his hand. His team at Yale, which he captained in his senior year playing third base, went twice to the NCAA championship finals, losing first to California, then to Southern Cal. He turned the baseball in his palm, enjoying the feel of it. "Nowadays the only time I handle these is throwing out ceremonial balls." He began describing an embarrassing moment when, hampered by a bulletproof vest, he had bounced a ball halfway to the Houston Astros catcher. "You tend to forget the distance," he said. "It's a question of raising your sights. You learn. Next time it's going to be right on target."

As we came down the stairs, a small group was standing in the foyer. I recognized members of the White House staff: Dan Quayle, the vice-president-elect; John Sununu, the chief of staff; Nick Brady, the secretary of the Treasury; and Brent Scowcroft, the national security adviser. Apparently the president-elect had scheduled a staff meeting. The toe of my stocking hung over a step. Sununu seemed to know something about my career as a participatory journalist. "Hey," he called up merrily. "A new cabinet member?"

The president-elect went to the door with me. As I stepped back into my loafers he urged me to come back for a rematch. He said that as soon as possible a horseshoe court was going to be installed at the White House. "When the horseshoe court is ready, there'll be a ribbon-cutting ceremony. Got to come down for that."

I said I would. "But," I said, "I'm bringing my own cowboy hat next time."

■ ■ ■

ON THE PLANE trip back to New York, thinking back on the horseshoe match, I remembered the Duke of Wellington's remark that the only thing to compare with the melancholy of a battle lost was that of a battle won. I wasn't so sure—at least not in this case. The president-elect was probably at this very moment leaning forward out of his chair at the Naval Observatory, chortling with delight and telling Quayle, Sununu, Scowcroft, Brady, and the rest of them what fun it had been—that he'd really cleaned that fellow's clock.

I began murmuring to myself. What had gone wrong? Probably I had let sympathy creep into my mind. I wasn't mentally prepared to apply the finishing measure—the killer instinct was missing, what I had heard called the X Factor, the ingredient that produced winners. Certainly *he* had it: witness that last extraordinary shot ("remember Iowa!"); witness that even such an insignificant act as throwing a ceremonial ball to a catcher had been evaluated: the next time he would raise his sights so that it would be right on target.

I began to feel sorry for myself. Shabby coat. I could feel the leather of my shoe with my toe through the hole in my sock. Things hadn't been going well elsewhere. The literary magazine, *The Paris Review*, which I have headed since its founding in the early 1950s, had lost money yet again—for the thirty-fifth straight year. Was there a connection— losing here, losing there?

What was needed, I decided, was a revamping, a reevaluation. The symbolic nexus was the horseshoe match. The president-elect had asked me to come to Washington to play him again. Perhaps in the interim, a change in attitude could be effected, a leaf turned, a new being constituted—competitive, confident, practical: a winner! I ordered a drink.

One course of action, naturally, would be to persuade my fellow tenants in New York City to let me set up a horseshoe court on the roof or in the cellar somewhere, so that I could practice day after day and perhaps even bring in a horseshoe expert for some coaching, who after a week or so would proclaim, "Hey, hey, now we're getting somewhere." But somehow that did not seem quite in the spirit of things: the president, occupied with the national debt by then, world crises here and there, and presumably (though one could never tell) unable to get down to the Rose Garden or wherever the horseshoe pit was going to be built, would not be able to keep his hand in.

Much more appropriate would be to prepare myself psychologically. I would ask advice of sports psychologists, Zen masters, motivators, gurus, people who had been enormously successful in other fields, corporate CEOs, general managers, coaches, topflight athletes, and, pumped up with what they had been able to offer, I would arrive in Washington (with a new pair of socks) and try again.

The plane turned and I could see the lights of New York. I felt more cheerful. The humiliation had begun to slip away. The man next to me had pulled a fedora over his eyes to keep the light out and had fallen asleep. He would want to hear that I had been playing horseshoes with the president-elect. I cleared my throat loudly.

2

FEW DAYS LATER I telephoned a good friend, Gene Scott, one of the great athletes Yale University has produced—a nine-letter man (in soccer, hockey, and tennis), a member of the Davis Cup team, and the successful editor-publisher of *Tennis Week*. Perhaps he would have some ideas about preparing for the rematch. He knew Bush. He had played tennis with him. We could chat about the X Factor.

Billy Talbert, the tennis star, was the first person I ever heard use that term. In Paris, in the 1950s, somebody had asked him what constituted winning a championship. He replied that an X Factor was involved. Pressed on what that meant, he said he was using the word to describe a quality beyond natural gifts. In a close match, the outcome is determined by only 3 or 4 points, what he called "swing points," and the winner of these points, Talbert said, is usually endowed with this mysterious component.

Added to the player's natural ability, it provides a kind of boost, like an afterburner kicking in. Talbert himself was the embodiment of the X Factor—slight, not especially fast, certainly not overpowering, and yet through savvy, spirit, and determination he had run up an astonishing record. He had won three national championships and, with different partners (usually Gardnar Mulloy or Tony Trabert), had won thirty-five championships in doubles.

When I reached Scott I said, "Guess what I've just run into. An X Factor."

After a pause he asked, "What are you talking about?"

I described how I'd gone down to Washington and in the course of things had played horseshoes in a match with George Bush.

"He beat you."

"Yes."

"I'm not surprised."

"He had the X Factor."

"Of course."

"Well, it was close," I said. I asked him how I would have done if we'd played tennis.

"He'd have beaten you. Technically, you have a better game, but you don't have much confidence in it. Bush, on the other hand, has an opinion of his game that far exceeds his ability: he simply has the confidence and the belief that he will prevail."

He started in on an interesting list of tennis players who, like Bush, had a kind of psychic energy that made them better than the sum of their parts: "Bitsy Grant— 'the Giant-Killer,' they called him; Bobby Riggs, of course; Ted Schroeder. Schroeder was a player who was helpless in the backcourt, didn't like to play there, so he was forever charging the net on his own serve or chipping and charging on receipt of service—all of this especially effective on grass on which all the major events in those days were played."

"What about the modern era?" I asked.

"Michael Chang," Scott said after a pause. "He has no visible overpowering strengths. No volley. No backhand. No offensive attitudes. But he runs well. A good athlete with a great quantity of moxie. He looks across the net and wants nothing more than to cut these big guys down to size." He snapped his fingers. "Jimmy Connors, of course. Great example. Mechanically, the guy's not much. But from the very beginning he was pumped full of confidence by his mother and Bill Reardon."

Somewhat tentatively, I asked Scott if there was any quick road to achieving this giant-killer characteristic, this X Factor, this attitude.

He laughed and said that one possibility was to diminish my height (I am six-four). "Get small," he said. "One thing about being small is that you get sick and tired of losing, and you figuratively become tall as a consequence. Of course," he said, "it's better if you're born with that X Factor you were speaking of." From the rueful way he mentioned it, I could tell he felt that my getting small was the only solution.

Scott was right about my tennis. I once described it as follows: I think I'm really quite a decent tennis player despite a perceptible hitch in the backhand stroke that causes the ball to float alarmingly, a serve that rests right on the edge of hysteria, a dismaying tactical sense that calls for the grandstand rather than the percentage shot (a drop shot executed from the baseline is one of my favorites), a running style that has something of the giraffe in it, and, above all, a morbid preoccupation during play with impending doom. Still, when the local yacht club tennis tournament rolls around in the last weeks of June, I enter it with an optimist's conviction that the opposition will be doing well to take a set from me as I move through the draw to the Fourth of July finals. The club has 197 members. The men's singles trophy, a Revere silver bowl, sits on the clubroom table. It is the smallest model Tiffany's offers, and one would be hard-pressed to load it up with more than seven or eight cashew nuts. I stare at it longingly. The runner-up trophy stands alongside. It is a fluted vase appropriate for a single long-stemmed rose, too thin for a name as lengthy as mine to be engraved on it without running back into itself. It shines its pristine polished light, however, and I persuade myself to find it acceptable if, by some chance . . .

My opponent in the first round is a tall, melancholy man who comes down to the courts carrying two aluminum rackets in their covers. During the warm-up his strokes are classic. Years of lessons and practice. I think of him as a mirror of myself. I had begun when I was eight— all those years on my grandparents' court with the apple basket of old tennis balls, trying to hit the handkerchief spread in the center of the service court. ("He aces Budge!" my inner voice exclaimed.) My grandmother had a parrot that flew around the place, untrammeled. Its favorite perch was the wire backstop, where it teetered in the soft winds, its tail hanging down behind. It enjoyed the tennis and the only phrase it uttered, which it did constantly, was "love–40!"

My opponent begins to practice his serve. His mouth goes ajar as he hits it. He had played on the team at Amherst, I had heard. Very shy man. Low voice. Asks if I am ready. The match begins. He wins the toss and double-faults. He double-faults again. He begins to disintegrate. My serve. His first return of service hits the net in the adjacent court. "Bend your knees, you fat faggot!" he cries at himself. His rage mounts. "Oh suffering Jesus!" he cries. We play appalling tennis and I extinguish him. We meet at the net. "I played well today," I say. I have read somewhere that Rod Laver uses that phrase when he walks up to the net to comfort his defeated opponents. The Amherst man detests me. I say, "Your game was a little off. I'd hate to run into it when it's on." He grunts. A very pretty girl who has been watching turns out to be his wife. She comes out on the court and touches his hand. She has olive eyes and high cheekbones. She loathes me. They get into a very expensive car. They are going to a grand lunch somewhere. I stare after them.

Second round: the day is muggy. My opponent is a sandy-haired older man who wears a hearing aid. He is one of the club's best yachtsmen. He came in third in the Bermuda Race one year. He wears blue yachting sneakers and khaki shorts. His tennis style is awkward. He pushes at the ball. During the warm-up I do not make an error. The match begins. After ten minutes he is ahead 3–0. He is steady. Everything comes back. I tighten up. I begin to play his game, patting the ball back. Rage begins to mount in me, first at him ("Why can't he *hit* the ball and play tennis like a man?") and then finally at myself. I berate myself, both verbally and physically. I cry out my name. I lift my racket and belt myself in the calf. A welt rises and throbs. He wins the first set. Play begins in the second. I net an easy volley. I refer to myself as an ox. The match is over. Nearly weeping with frustration, I walk to the net. Is he going to say something? He is. "I was really on today," he says. He puts out his hand. I murmur my apologies for having played so badly. "Can I buy you a ginger ale or something?" he asks.

"Not for me," I say. I have a terrible thirst.

He waves his racket airily and says he must rush off. The starting gun is less than an hour away. Off he goes to beat somebody up on the waters of the Sound.

I go to my car. I am perspiring heavily. I stick to the seats. I think about the X Factor. Why hadn't it turned up? Why was it out yachting, or whatever? I wonder if I'll be able to stand the country-club buffet that night. The guy with the tall chef's hat standing behind the roast beef platter, he will know. I turn the ignition key. The motor hums. I put the top down. The wind will feel nice on the skin. I begin to feel a bit better. They are having a picnic on the rocks by Seal Head. They'll have brought ice-cold lemonade down in thermos bottles.

Still, I will brood about what happened. I have never dared to admit to myself that perhaps physical failings—a quirky eye, a lack of speed, for example—might be the reason for my troubles. The dream of winning the country-club trophy would evaporate if I allowed myself to believe such heresy. The root of my troubles, I have always told myself, has been largely mental—a tendency to collapse in the face of adversity and succumb to a state of what was once known in tennis as "getting it in the elbow," stiffening up, choking, as in my match with the elderly gentleman with the hearing aid. Consequently, I have always been fascinated by the mental devices used to stave off such terrors. For years one of my favorite players was Art Larsen, who was the U.S. champion in 1950. He had returned to tennis on the advice of a psychiatrist as therapy for a series of breakdowns caused by war duty. Larsen worked up a most interesting mental device, or catalyst, for himself—a large imaginary eagle that would float above the court like a reconnaissance plane, and then between points come down to perch on his shoulder to advise and cajole him through a match. Larsen had a habit one noticed after a while: just before serving, he would twist his head slightly, ostensibly to listen to what the eagle had to say.

Envying Larsen his eagle, for a while I tried a more massive extension of his device: while playing, I imagined that I was being watched and advised by a gallery of spectators bunched together in a box at courtside who, on occasion, in disregard of tennis etiquette, would offer sharp cries of encouragement or disgust. In the box were Ernest Hemingway; King Gustav of Sweden, the ancient who played tennis into his nineties; Marianne Moore, the poet fascinated in her quirky way by athletic skills; Dwight Davis of the Davis Cup; Gottfried von Cramm, the German Davis-Cupper, I have no idea why, but there he is; Bitsy (the Giant-Killer) Grant; my grandmother and her parrot; Art Larsen's eagle; Brigitte Bardot; Ezra Pound, another poet who was a tennis enthiusiast and played with Hemingway in Paris in the twenties; Allison Danzig, the tennis writer for the *New York Times*; and a few others I associated with tennis. Sometimes in this group of shimmering faces others were discernible, especially when things were going badly: at the back of the box General Aleksandr Samsonov, who lost the battle of Tannenberg, one of the most disastrous of military defeats in history, appears, and along with him, Captain Edward J. Smith of the *Titanic*. Things don't go well after these two put in an appearance and they begin to elbow their way down into the front seats.

■ ■ ■

EVERYONE MUST WONDER wistfully if there isn't something other than what they actually practice in their lives (playing in a yacht-club tennis tournament) at which they would be incredibly adept if they could only find out what it was—that a paintbrush worked across a canvas for the first time would indicate an amazing talent. Or that one would rise from a minor position at the executive board meeting table and address the CEOs with a proposal so illuminating that around the rim of the mahogany table the officers of the company would rise and applaud. If an idiot savant could sit down at a piano and suddenly bat out a Chopin etude, wasn't the same sort of potential locked up somewhere in all of us?

I have always wondered (less so, I must admit, as the years have gone by) if there wasn't some extraordinary athletic skill lurking within my body of which I was not aware—as if by chance on some athletic field I had picked up a javelin and thrown it, just to try, and through some perfect and startling alchemic convulsion of muscles the thing had sailed an eighth of a mile and stuck quivering in the earth. Astonished observers would ask to see it done again. Why not? After a few more titanic tosses, just to show that a fluke was not involved and of course surprising myself in the process, I would be urged to call the U.S. Olympic Committee. "Ahem," I planned to say when I got an authority on the line, "I've just discovered the most extraordinary thing about myself. I am a javelin thrower."

Unlike others who share such absurd Walter Mitty daydreams, I had actually done something about it. A month before the Olympic Games in 1984, I had gone to the Olympic Training Center under the shadow of Pike's Peak in Colorado Springs to be tested in the sports physiology laboratories to see if by chance there was a particular Olympic event (after all, there are over 200 of them) for which I was perfectly adapted. I planned to write a piece about their findings.

A number of teams were in training at the Center when I arrived. I looked at them speculatively—judo (no chance there—too specialized), boxing (no, wrong-shaped nose), race-walkers (not dignified enough on the move), water-polo players, their nose clips dangling from their necks (a possibility?), and then out above the training fields I spotted the occasional arc of a javelin on the wing.

My testers were Dr. Jackie Puhl, a young vibrant woman with a Ph.D. in exercise physiology from Kent State, who rides a bicycle ten miles a day to her job at the Center, and Bob Hintermeister, a lean sprinter type who earned his degree in physical education at the University of Massachusetts. Dr. Puhl said: "A lot of what we can offer from here is a kind of support system for your coach so he can get a theoretical optimization of your athletic abilities."

"I don't have a coach," I said.

"Oh."

After a pause, I said, "Maybe I can get a coach after you tell me what I can do best."

I spent the day moving from one instrument to the next. I sat down and pulled at the sawed-off oars of a Concept II rowing ergometer. I submitted myself to a Bio-kinetic Pacer bench unit. I performed on a Quinton 18-72 treadmill, breathing hard into a hoselike attachment called a Gould programmable electric ergometer. At each

station, computer screens glowed with figures, and printouts emerged, many with finely etched graphs. I was
strapped into the Cybex II isokinetic dynamometer to
measure the strength of my arms and legs. The Cybex (I
was told) can show if an athlete has a muscle imbalance—
whether the right leg is stronger than the left, in which
case the balance can be redressed with the proper exercise. "This will tell if I tilt when I walk," I said. "Possibly," Mr. Hintermeister said.

The first indication of excitement on the part of my
testers came with an exercise called the fev 1.0, which
measures how much air can be forcefully blown out in
one second. Fev 1.0 stands for Forced Expiratory Volume
at one second.

"It is really a very sharp curve," Hintermeister said,
looking at the graph. "It's almost as if . . . you blew up
balloons for a living." He looked at me questioningly.

"Well, I blow up the usual four or five a year," I told
him. "Birthday parties. I can tell you that the cheaper the
balloon the more difficult it is to inflate. The really cheap
ones tend to escape the lips and flail around the room.
Right?"

One test I skipped—which was to have some muscle
removed to tell whether I was a slow or fast twitcher. I
didn't like the looks of the instrument that does this—a
cylinder about the size of a large fountain pen. It contains
a guillotine-like contraption that snips off a piece of muscle so its fibers can be inspected through a microscope.
The procedure leaves a small scar, perhaps a centimeter in
length. What is learned by going through this is whether
one has a high percentage of fast-twitch muscle fibers,
which means one's muscular makeup is suitable for anae-
robic activities such as weight lifting or the 100-yard dash,

where gulps of oxygen are not at a premium, or slow-twitch, which indicates aerobic activities in which lungs full of oxygen are required, such as kayaking or running a marathon.

I have since regretted not having this done—if only for the scar. A scar, even a small one that must be searched for, is worth having for conversational gambits. "See this here. Got it trying out for the Olympics. Showed I was a fast [or slow] twitcher."

At the end of my session Jackie Puhl collected the printouts and the data sheets and we gathered around a conference table. "Have any patterns emerged?" I asked. "There are," Dr. Puhl replied, "two interesting oddities about your charts." My heart jumped.

"First of all, which is very unusual, your hamstrings—that is to say the muscles in the back of your thighs—are far more powerful than the quadricep muscles in the front, those four muscular bands we call quads. Very unusual."

"What does it mean?"

"It means that you can kick backwards more powerfully than you can kick forward."

"Oh."

"Then your fev 1.0 test," Dr. Puhl went on, "shows that you're very adept at expelling air swiftly. Snorting."

"What is this good for? Does an Olympic event come to mind?"

"This backward kicking motion might come in handy riding a horse," Dr. Puhl said. "Spurring him on."

Hintermeister came up with a comment. "It's too bad football isn't on the Olympic agenda," he said. "You could kick field goals backwards."

Dr. Puhl shuffled her papers and continued. "As for

being able to blow out sharply, I just don't know. With swimmers, of course, it's helpful to be able to exhale abruptly, but the rest of your tests don't suggest the water's your medium. I'm quite at a loss, frankly."

Some months later a somewhat caustic friend of mine—to whom I had described the Colorado Springs findings—was ingeniuous enough to offer an activity that smartly combined both skills. "That combination of kicking backward, pawing at the ground," he said, "and snorting sharply, brings only one thing to mind. And that's the bullfight." He paused. "That's where you belong, the bullring, and it's not the matador I have in mind!"

3

THE X FACTOR is obviously of extraordinary, even morbid, interest not only to sports journalists like myself, but to general managers, coaches, athletes, and indeed the general public. What *is* the ingredient that makes one athlete considerably better than another, though both are of equivalent physical skills? Even more mysterious, what is it that makes an entire team better than another when the general makeup of each is about the same?

I had a series of conversations on the subject with Bill Curry, an All-Pro center in the 1970s and a successful coach at Georgia Tech, Alabama, and now the University of Kentucky. I got to know him when I was doing a participatory-journalism stint with the Baltimore Colts.

He pointed out that the X Factor was much easier to define in individuals. One example of a player who had it was Willie Davis, the great defensive end at Green Bay where Curry played his rookie year before going to the

Colts. One afternoon Davis had given him a kind of mental tip that he used to motivate himself. He had used it ever since a game the Packers lost against the Eagles back in the 1960s. As he left the field at the end of the game, Davis had turned around, the stands emptying, and he realized that he was leaving something on the field— namely, regrets that he had not given the extra effort, the extra push . . . and that he was going to have to live with that regret for the rest of his life because there was no way that he could recapture that moment. He made up his mind then that he would never again look back at a football field or even a day's effort at what he was doing with any sense of regret. Curry described watching Packer game films when the outcome was long decided and how he always marveled at Davis's white-heat intensity throughout, never dogging it or taking it easy.

"It may be that small moment in his life which provided him with his X Factor."

"What about the X Factor with teams?" I asked.

"It all begins with the players having the capacity to focus," Curry said. "Without that, it just never happens. When I was a child I was fascinated by these little magnifying glasses—I'd get them out of Cracker Jack boxes. I could sit in the woods on a day when it was 35 degrees, and with the sun 93 million miles away I could be involved in a process that brought the rays that distance and centered them with a magnifying glass on one spot until a pile of leaves would burst into flame. A focus of energy. Everybody who has this X Factor has the capacity to zero in so totally. If you've ever looked at a picture of Bjorn Borg hitting a ball, look at his eyes. Ted Williams picking up the actual stitches on the baseball.

"So what I teach our teams is that you've got to focus

on the task. Then I go on to give them the five characteristics of every great overachieving person I've ever studied. We teach these almost every day . . . to the staff, the team, anybody who'll listen."

He raised a finger.

"Number one—it really doesn't matter if it's Helen Keller or Wilma Rudolph or Vince Lombardi—is a kind of singleness of purpose. You see it when that little squirt Michael Chang goes on the court to hit a tennis ball. There's such a singleness of purpose that everything else is blocked out—the crowd noise, the weather conditions, the fact that the other guy can hit BBs and you can't—it doesn't matter; you're going to beat him anyhow. That's the first characteristic. The second is unselfishness. The capacity to give when other people won't or can't. When your legs won't move another step, somehow you make a move. In a team effort, it's the capacity to create the win with absolutely no concern for who gets the credit. It's an attitude that is just as applicable to business. In college I was an industrial-management major at Georgia Tech, which has turned out an astonishing number of CEOs who are among *Fortune* magazine's top 500. The chairmen of the boards of Delta, American Express, Phillips Petroleum—all those guys went to Georgia Tech. These are the ingredients that I found in those people: the ability to convey a sense of family and caring and concern with all different kinds of personalities. It comes with the leader being willing to serve, being willing to make himself the least. He walks in at six o'clock in the morning and makes the janitor feel important; he does unselfish things."

I mentioned that greed and selfishness were increasingly associated with business.

"Greed is not in my quotient," Curry said, "unless you define greed in an altruistic way, meaning every action is in a sense selfish. If Mother Teresa gets a warm feeling from feeding a starving child in India, she is being rewarded. She's not interested in making a million dollars, but she gets her reward. But if greed is defined as the accumulation of wealth for its own sake, that's the opposite of what we're talking about. One guy with that kind of motive can destroy a whole team. The Boston Celtics come down the court and if Larry Bird wanted to shoot all the time, the Celtics wouldn't have won all those championships. Bird can't jump, he can't run; the guy is a country boy. But when he gets on the court, he becomes magic because he is unselfish."

"What's the third characteristic?" I asked.

"Toughness. A champion is tough. But I don't mean gritting your teeth, foaming at the mouth, and hitting people on the side of the head. I mean being honest in your effort when other people are not being honest. Sticking to the principles of fair play and ethical behavior and outconditioning, outthinking, outworking your opponent rather than finding ways to bend the rules. That is real toughness, at least in the NCAA today. The real tough guys are able to suck it up and follow the rules, even when they're getting pasted. The gutless ones, the ones who are not tough, are the ones who have to break the rules to win; they aren't winners at all—in fact, they've never won a single match. When you commit a dishonest act, you lose power. When you refuse to denigrate yourself, there is a great power, a great X Factor, that accrues to your benefit. Norman Vincent Peale called it the Plus Factor. Homer Rice, the athletic director at Georgia Tech, calls it the Inner Power Success Force.

"The fourth characteristic I've found is that all champions are smart. It has nothing to do with IQ, with education. I don't know quite how to say it except that it's street smart, country smart . . . they just know their business. Certain people, like John Unitas or Bart Starr, come out of the huddle on the football field and, if you had to play against them, you'd know you were going to be cut to ribbons. It's partly intuitive, but it's also part training. It's knowing your business.

"The fifth one's the most important. Champions never quit. Sometimes I get up in front of the team and I say, 'Did you ever get in a fistfight with a guy you thought you were going to beat up really easily and you knock him down, turn to walk away, and you realize he's gotten up, and you knock him down, and the son of a gun gets up again, and it starts to dawn on you that this is going to be a long day? Before long, you're not knocking him down anymore; he's knocking you down. You've gotten in a fight with the wrong guy. He's not gonna quit.' Then it becomes a battle of the wills—like the old-time boxing matches when you had to put your toe to the line and they went 139 rounds. That was the ultimate contest: who would quit first. I remember an interviewer asking John McEnroe about Connors one time: 'What is it about Jimmy Connors?' McEnroe thought about it, and he said, 'You can beat him a hundred times in a row and he'll never admit it.' Lombardi said, 'I've never lost a game.' We thought he was nuts. Then we realized he meant that the clock ran out on him. His attitude never changed. He said, 'Winning is not the most important thing; it is the only thing.' When he elaborated on that he'd go on to say, 'Winning is not the most important thing; the *will to win* is the most important.' The game clock may run out, but the will continues.

"So, in short, champions have the capacity to focus; they have a singleness of purpose. They are unselfish— able to give when others can't and when there's no apparent reward. They are tough—meaning tough endurance-wise but also meaning willing to follow the rules when the competition will not; they are smart; and they just never quit. I think it goes across the board: business, politics, sports, life."

I told Curry that I planned to play President Bush in a game of horseshoes. A win was rather important. Did he have any practical advice?

He thought for a while. "Well, if I were going to play with the president of the United States, I would lose," he said with a grin, " . . . out of respect and awe for the office."

"I already have," I said. "We have a rematch coming up."

"Oh. Well, it depends how badly you want to win," Curry said. "If it's a social event, then I'd relax and not think about it. I'd play and I'd have fun. If you're into the X Factor thing you've been talking about, I'd get the best videotape there is on horseshoe pitching, study it, drill yourself. I'd visualize beating the president—the horseshoes coming down on the stake, seeing the score the way you want it, shaking hands with him. It will happen because you saw it in your mind. I'd call in the great experts. We bring in Jan Stenerud to work with our kickers, Joe Namath and Bart Starr to rub shoulders with the quarterbacks . . . see if they can instill the X Factor."

"And is that possible?" I asked.

"Sometimes," he said. "Of course, that's the fascinating thing about the X Factor. Each person has his own . . . a potential; so in that sense it's indefinable. . . . "

■ ■ ■

BILL CURRY'S COACH at Green Bay had been Vince Lombardi. We talked about him once—surely the exemplar of someone who could bestow the X Factor quotient on an entire team. Curry had said: "The key to him was that he believed that you win not by systems or superstar players but by execution. So a player had to suffer the consequences of being driven to execute. Everything was directed at that. It was brilliantly simple. In fact, the technical part of football was much simpler than I thought it was going to be—the simplest of all the systems I played under. When I first got to Green Bay, Ken Bowman, who was the other center, went through all the plays with me in one afternoon. Then the next day, Lombardi himself sat down with me and on one sheet of a legal pad he drew up every single play that the Green Bay players had. I think of all the documents, the awards, all the memorabilia of my career, and I'd give them up for that one sheet of paper, which I lost, or never thought was worth keeping. The famous one on the paper, of course, was the power sweep. Lombardi's theory was that nobody could stop the power sweep without giving away something else. There was no need for any fancy deception or anything of that sort in his way of thinking. We had a reverse in our playbook. I don't think we ever ran it while I was there.

"Of course, it wasn't just the technical part that made the Packers great. The difficult thing is to articulate how really forceful Lombardi's presence was. Jerry Kramer didn't get it in his book *Instant Replay*. He just didn't capture it. No one has. They did a TV show with Ernest Borgnine and it was just pathetic. Borgnine wasn't pathetic—Borgnine was superb. But they decided the Lombardi story was about a man going from New York, where he'd hoped to be a head coach, to an obscure town in northern Wisconsin that his wife didn't like. Crazy. The real story should have been about this man's ability to shock, to frighten, to overpower people with whatever means he had to use. On the first day he gathered the team together, he always showed the film of the championship game the year before. He didn't comment on it; he just showed it, whether the Packers were in it or not. And then he'd turn off the projector and he'd say, 'Gentlemen, I have no illusions about what's going to happen to me if I don't win. So don't you have any illusions about what's going to happen if you don't produce for me. . . . There are three things that are important in your life: your religion, your family, and the Green Bay Packers—in that order.' And then, as soon as we'd get down there on the field, he'd get the order mixed up in his own mind. What was paramount was—by whatever means—to build in you the sense that you had to be the best ever. When I first came to pro ball I just wanted to make the team; then when I did, I decided I sure would like to be first string; then after that I made All-Pro, and I thought: Now I want to be All-Pro every year. The obsession to be the best was precisely Lombardi's. Time and time again he'd say things like this: 'When you go on the field, I want you to think about one thing—that is, for this day I'm going to be the greatest center in football. When those people walk out of the stands, I want that guy to turn to his wife and say, "We just saw the greatest offensive center who ever played." '

"So he had this canny talent for manipulating people to be exactly what he wanted them to be. He would select a role for each player. He wrote the play, he did the choreography, and if you didn't fit the role, he would change your personality so that you could play the part. If you didn't like the role, it didn't make any difference; he manipulated you and made you what he wanted you to be until you could play it better than anybody else in the National Football League. *Or* he would get rid of you. I heard him tell Steve Wright, who was a guy who grinned a lot—he'd miss a block and come back to the huddle with a smile on his face, which would drive Lombardi insane. 'Goddammit, Wright, you think that's funny! You're never gonna be a man! You're never gonna make it! *Yes,* you are! *I'm* gonna make you, I'm gonna create you. I'm gonna make you into something before I'm through with you.' "

"What do you truly think he thought of all you players?" I asked.

Curry thought for a while, and then he said, "This will be argued by some players, but I believe that Lombardi really did love us. I don't think he could've appealed to our better instincts if we didn't feel that he really cared about us. I've seen him cry when we lost a game. It wasn't for appearance's sake. I mean, I've just seen the tears in his eyes. Of course, it was foremost because *he* had lost. But he also had genuine affection for . . . he liked to be around 'the guys.' He wanted to be accepted. When he was admonishing us about our behavior, he used to say things to us like: 'Don't you think that I'd like to go get drunk downtown too? Don't you think I'd like to go out and do that? Don't you think I'd like you guys to like me? I know you don't like me. But I don't give a crap about that. We're here to do a job. Your liking me is not near as important as winning football games. So I don't *care* if you like me.' That kind of thing. Every now and then it would surface, but it was very rare. He was such an odd contradiction. He was very profane, yet he went to church every day; he was a daily celebrant, Catholic, very devout. He considered the priesthood at one point. Bart Starr said, 'When I heard about this man taking over the team in 1959, I could hardly wait to meet a man that went to church every day.' Then he went on to say, 'I worked for him for two weeks and then I realized this man *needs* to go to church every day.' "

"Didn't anybody stand up to him?"

"We had a sort of war council," Curry said, "in which there were about six guys—Bob Skoronski, who was the offensive captain, and Tom Moore and Bart and Paul Hornung, guys like that—and every now and then when things got really bad, about once a year, they'd go to Lombardi and say, 'Coach, you're going to have to let up. You're driving us all crazy! We can't function under this withering kind of abuse.' Maybe he'd let up for a day or two. Maybe we'd have a good game, and he'd be nice for a few days. But then we'd have a bad game, and he'd stomp back in on Tuesday morning and everybody'd just be sitting there aquiver. He'd say, 'I tried it your way. I'm sick and tired of being father confessor for a bunch of yellow, no-good punks. The whip! That's the only thing you understand. And I'm going to whip you again, and drive you, make you! Why do I always have to make you? Don't you think I get tired of being this way?' Once again everybody would squirm and feel that somehow they'd made the wrong choice for a profession: What am I doing with this person here? Why? But invariably he would come back in the next breath and win everybody over again . . . although sometimes you couldn't imagine how he could do it.

"Once in 1965 we had been to Los Angeles and had lost a game to the Rams that we *had* to win. Los Angeles was the last-place team in the league and they just *stomped* us. On the way back, Lionel Aldridge—the big defensive end—began to sing. A couple of beers and he was singing! Lombardi heard about it. Well, on Tuesday morning he came into the meeting and he began to question Lionel's ancestry. He got into such an emotional shouting binge that it was like one of those tirades you'd see in films of Hitler going through a frenzy—though I don't mean to draw any parallel. I'm talking about awesome, forceful personalities, not the quality of what they did or the kind of people they were. Finally Lombardi said, 'I want all the assistant coaches out of this room and all the doors shut. I want to be here with these football players . . . if that's what you can call them.' So everybody cleared out. Scurried out."

"The assistant coaches?" I asked.

"Oh yes. The assistant coaches were terrified of him too. Absolutely. You could hear him in the next room dressing *them* down the same way he did us, though of course he never did it in front of us.

"When the coaches were out and the doors were shut, Lombardi really went at it. The meeting seemed to go on for an hour and a half, with Lombardi screaming, shouting: 'Goddammit, you guys don't care if you win or lose. I'm the only one that cares. I'm the only one that puts his blood and his guts and his heart into the game! You guys show up, you listen a little bit, you concentrate . . . you've got the concentration of three-year-olds. You're nothing! I'm the only guy that gives a damn if we win or lose.'

"Suddenly there was a stirring in the back of the room, a rustle of chairs. I turned around and there was Forrest Gregg, on his feet, bright red, with a player on either side, holding him back by each arm, and he was straining forward. Gregg was another real gentlemanly kind of guy, very quiet. Great football player. Lombardi looked at him and stopped. Forrest said, 'Goddammit, Coach . . . excuse me for the profanity.' Even at his moment of rage he was still both respectful enough and intimidated enough that he stopped and apologized. Then he went on: ''Scuse the language, Coach, but it makes me sick to hear you say something like that. We lay it on the line for you every Sunday. We live and die the same way you do, and it hurts.' Then he began straining forward again, trying to get up there to punch Lombardi out. Players were holding him back. Then Bob Skoronski stood up, very articulate. He was the captain of the team. 'That's right,' he said. 'Dammit, don't you tell us that we don't care about winning. That makes me sick. Makes me want to puke. We care about it every bit as much as you do. It's our knees and our bodies out there that we're throwing around.'

"So there it was. The coach had been confronted, the captain of a ship facing a mutinous crew, with the first mate standing and staring him down face-to-face, and it truly looked as though he had lost control of the situation.

"But then damned if the master didn't triumph again. After just a moment's hesitation he said, 'All right. Now *that's* the kind of attitude I want to see. Who else feels that way?'

"Well, at this very moment Willie Davis was nervously rocking back and forth on his metal folding chair. Willie was known as Dr. Feelgood on the team because every day at practice, with everybody limping around and tired and moaning and complaining, somebody always looked over, and asked, 'Willie, how you feel?' He always said the same thing: 'Feel *good*, man!' So there was Dr. Feelgood rocking back and forth and you know how those chairs are. He lost his balance and he fell forward! He fell right out into the middle of the room . . . onto his feet; it looked as if he had leapt from his chair just as Lombardi asked, 'Who else feels that way?' And Willie sort of grinned sheepishly and he said, 'Yeah, me, too! I feel that way, man!' Lombardi said, 'All right, Willie, that's great.' And it swept through the room; everybody said, 'Yeah, hell—me too!' and suddenly you had forty guys that could lick the world. That's what Lombardi created out of that situation. He went around to each player in that room with the exception of the rookies—he skipped the four of us rookies—and as he looked in each man's face he said, 'Do you want to win football games for me?' And the answer was 'Yes, sir'—forty times. He wended his way through that mass of people sitting around in that disarray of chairs and looked at each guy nose-to-nose two inches from his face and he said that same thing: 'Do you want to win football games?' and every man said, 'Yes, sir,' and we did not lose another game that year."

4

B

Y CHANCE I ran into Willie Davis, the great Green Bay
defensive end Bill Curry had been talking about. Since his
football days he has become a CEO, sits on a number of
important boards, and is considered as fine a businessman
as he was a football player.

I asked Davis if his years at Green Bay had been of any
value to him afterward. He laughed. "Lombardi," he
said. "I think the majority of us quickly identified the
qualities we learned at Green Bay as being the keys to any
success afterward. Lombardi often referred to the bridge
between what we were doing for him and what came
after. He would say to us, 'If you don't do it here, you're
not going to turn it on in another life. If you can prove
here what it takes to get it done, the next job is not going
to be that different.' "

Davis went on to say that sports create a kind of arena
in which you get a lot of quick answers—not only about

yourself but about other people. Sports provide a kind of laboratory in which you can see how others perform under stress, playing out emotions, working toward a goal. "The basics in business," he said, "are really very similar."

I asked if Lombardi would have made a good CEO. Davis laughed again and said that yes, he thought so. "He would always set a good example. Tough as he was on others, he was always prepared to do the same himself. You'd go by his office in Green Bay at midnight and you'd see his car parked outside the office. He was in there working. That was one of the impressions he left: Do as I do. Not just as I say."

"Willie," I asked, "do you remember a play in Philadelphia? Bill Curry described it to me once. . . ."

"Oh, yes," Davis said. "The moment of commitment. It was late in the third quarter. Billy Barnes made a great run around the other end. When the play started out I knew I could get over there to him and bring him down— I'd done it before—but then I began thinking, why overextend myself? There were other Packers over there. They could handle it. So I moved over there kind of casual, and there goes Barnes for 25, 30 yards. It was an important run because it was a third-down situation.

"Well, that play stuck in my mind. Indelible. If I'd gone at first opportunity, there's no doubt I would've reached Barnes and got him down. No doubt. Maybe we wouldn't have won the game, but I told myself that never again would I come out of a situation wondering if I could have done a job better. It's just as important to me today as it was then. Every day that's what I tell myself—not to let an opportunity slide by that I could have taken advantage of."

■ ■ ■

IT WAS AN interesting parallel to consider—sports and business. I brought it up in a conversation with Anthony O'Reilly, who is the head of H.J. Heinz Company. He was a great rugby player in the 1950s and '60s, star of Ireland, winner in his country of the equivalent of the Heisman Trophy. He loves the game of rugby with a great passion. Indeed, on one occasion he came out of retirement to play, long after he should have, but then vowed he would not do so again after his captain told him that his best effort against the opposing players had been to shake his jowls at them.

Outspoken, his voice a rich, rolling brogue one might associate with the Dublin Players theater group, he turned out, very much like Willie Davis, to be a firm believer in the close correlation between sports and big business. In fact, three of the businesses he is involved in besides Heinz (a multinational newspaper company, an oil-and-gas exploration company, and an industrial holding group) have in their operations people who played rugby with him.

"They all exhibit very much the characteristics in their daily business lives that they did on the rugby field," he told me. "Those who were terriers on the rugby field turned out to be terriers in business. If you determine what business is all about and what the characteristics are that bring people to the top of the business pile, I think you'll find that a great parallel exists, especially in the competitive team sports. I don't find such parallels in the individual sports. Indeed, many of the characteristics in those—for example, John McEnroe—would probably suggest a disqualification."

"You don't imagine McEnroe as a CEO?"

"I see him, perhaps, as the CEO of his own company," O'Reilly said with a grin, "in which he is the only member of the board, arguing with himself."

Thinking of McEnroe, I couldn't resist asking O'Reilly about what seems the most undisciplined and unruly aspect of rugby—the scrum, that oddest of the sporting conformations, insectlike, the legs churning under a carapace of human backs.

"What's it like in there?" I asked.

"It sounds like a men's locker room," O'Reilly said. "A lot of unfriendly advice is given from one side to the other. The basic conflict is a law of applied physics, because eight men scrum down against eight men. You'll remember the definition of the game of rugby—that while soccer is a gentleman's game played by thugs, rugby is a thug's game played by gentlemen. In rugby, just as in American football, there is a high level of controlled violence, which tests you against a lot of life's basic instinctive reactions. It requires a great deal of communality at the higher level; you quickly have the whole notion of collegiality . . . that is, a sense of a group of people having a common purpose. You learn the acme of team sports—the subjugation of individual ambition to the common purpose. The selection procedure to put together a team has to be of the most rigorous kind, and the most ruthless: no nepotism, nobody's mommy or daddy or bank balance or what school one went to. It's a meritocracy out there on the rugby field, and that's the way a business should be run. If someone doesn't make it, you put him on the sidelines, or on the taxi squad, or get rid of him altogether."

O'Reilly railed against the star system that he felt was

an unfortunate part not only of American team sports but also of business. "There has to be a certain sublimation in all of this," he said. "In order for a team to be invincible, there's got to be collective skills rather than individual brilliance. The teams I played on had no great stars. The New Zealanders, the best of the internationals, had stars, but they were of the muted variety. In business, the level of political drama within a company is exacerbated by an excess adulation of one or two people—the cult of the personality. America is particularly adept at taking a man and using him as an icon to explain business. Lee Iacocca is a classic example. Seven years ago he was voted the best CEO in the country. He got three-quarters of the selection committee's votes. This year he got none. Now, does that mean he was better seven years ago than now? No. What happened seven years ago was a trigger mechanism and voluntary quotas put on the import of Japanese cars. So he was the beneficiary of protectionism. But now that's gone, his own costs have gone against him. I think that's an example of what can go wrong with a star system. Heinz is not Tony O'Reilly, and Chrysler is not Lee Iacocca. What games like football teach us is that you must have basic qualifications and an ongoing rigorous education toward a common cause . . . properly motivated and massively compensated through the reward system."

I asked him about Vince Lombardi and his quote about winning being the only thing.

"I reject it," O'Reilly said. "I absolutely reject it. It's vulgar. It carries the seeds of destruction." He went on to say that his favorite quote was from Kipling's "If," which used to hang above the player's entrance to center court at

Forest Hills: "If you can meet with Triumph and Disaster / And treat those two imposters just the same / . . . you'll be a Man, my son!"

"The amateur sports I played," O'Reilly said, "had that great Corinthian quality: we were playing for sport, and at the same time we were qualifying to be lawyers, doctors, dentists, and in the case of the Welsh, in that great democracy of players—bulldozer drivers, steel-workers, tin puddlers. One chap who was a bulldozer driver said to me one day, 'The trouble with you university chaps is that you use great long words like "corrugated" and "marmalade" '—the only two long words he could come up with. But if I were in Wales looking for someone to do something that required integrity, the first person I'd call would be Corrugated Marmalade himself, because I know I'd be getting 100 percent of what he had to offer."

"But you wouldn't ask him to be a CEO?"

"No. Well, I wouldn't put him into a debate with Mr. Kissinger."

He told a story that he felt illustrated the difference between the Corinthian attitudes of amateurism and the near-professionalism of collegiate sports in the United States. The famed American Peter Dawkins had turned up at Oxford on a Rhodes scholarship, preceded by an extraordinary reputation as an athlete—a great career at West Point as a running back, which had won him the Heisman Trophy. At Oxford he played rugby, though his position on the team for the traditional Oxford-Cambridge match at Twickenham was by no means assured. At both Oxford and Cambridge only the fifteen players picked to play in that game get their "blue," which is the equivalent of getting a varsity letter at an American college. To receive a blue (the color for both universities is blue—Oxford dark and Cambridge light) means much more in the British scheme of things than earning a letter does in the States. "He played football for Michigan," say, has a fine ring, but it doesn't compare to what it means in England to say, "He has his blue—rugby, y'know."

The team captain decides who is to play. At Oxford, the selection for the team takes place at a black-tie dinner at Balliol College during the week before the Tuesday on which the game is played every year.

"It was the contrast," O'Reilly said. "Here was Dawkins, who had gone through all the hoopla of the Heisman Trophy—radio, television, the huge press—standing rather nervously in his tuxedo, waiting to hear from the captain upstairs if he was going to be picked to play at Twickenham. It was not at all clear that he was good enough to get his blue.

"Well, the captain appeared from upstairs, picked out a dry sherry for himself, came over, and with that infuriating way the British have of looking at you as though they hadn't seen you for forty-two years, when in fact you've both been in the shower room a half-hour before, he said, 'Oh, Dawkins, there you are.' Then, referring to the Tuesday game, he said, 'Oh, by the way, Dawkins, are you free next Tuesday?' And that's how the Heisman Trophy winner learned he'd won his blue!

"Do you know who one of my favorite American heroes is," O'Reilly suddenly asked. "Frank Shields."

"The tennis player. . . . "

"Do you know the story of Shields and the French championships? Well, in 1931 Shields got into the finals of the tournament at Roland Garros. He'd had a very tough semifinal match . . . and he thought he'd relax from it at a party at the American embassy. There he met a pretty young girl who in the middle of all the celebrating announced that she had to leave the party to catch a train. She was on her way back to the United States. Frank gallantly took her to the Gare de Lyons to see her off, but then he got on the train with her . . . the boat train to Le Havre. The celebrating continued. When he woke up the next morning he looked out a porthole to discover he was a hundred miles out to sea. He lost the final by default."

O'Reilly roared with laughter. "Now that's heroic in my mind," he said. "Anybody can lose, but by Jove, to lose with such style . . . that's very convincing!"

■ ■ ■

ANOTHER HUGE COMPANY that disapproves of the star system so derided by Tony O'Reilly would surely be IBM. In fact, Thomas J. Watson, Jr., when he was the CEO, felt that IBM's astonishing resiliency was due not to the skill of its administrators (which I would have guessed) but to the power of its fundamental company guidelines. These were enunciated by the first of the Watsons, T. J. Sr., who joined IBM in 1914 when he was forty—having been fired as the general manager of National Cash Register Company and brought in to run a loose alliance of three small companies. The tenets can be put rather simply: to do every job well, to treat all people with dignity and respect, to appear neatly dressed, to be clear and forthright, to be eternally optimistic, and above all to be loyal. The various disciplines that evolved to sustain these family values are well known—a dress code (white shirts), no booze at company functions, among others.

At the same time, the Watsons always worried about

the stifling effect such codes and disciplines might have on an organization: they were very much in favor of what they called "wild ducks"—mavericks would be the contemporary term. Wild ducks was a description based on a Søren Kierkegaard story about a farmer who put out so much feed for the wild ducks that after four or five years they didn't bother migrating; they grew so fat and lazy that they found it difficult to fly at all—the point being that you can tame a wild duck, but you can't teach him to be wild again.

Whatever the Watsons felt about wild ducks, conformity has certainly left its mark on IBM. Some years ago at the Fontainbleau Hotel in Miami Beach, I was to give speeches to a succession of IBM salesmen—600 at a time—who were members of what was called the Gold Circle. For selling a certain amount of IBM equipment, the membership was rewarded by a vacation in Miami and various entertainments, of which listening to me was supposed to be one. In their dark suits, the sensible ties over the white shirts, the salesmen trooped into the convention theater of the hotel, a plush emporium with seats that had been equipped with push buttons so the audience could respond yes or no to questions asked of them, the tabulation in numbers flashing up on a huge screen behind the lectern on the stage. The IBM executives in charge of the meetings urged me to ask questions so that the buttons could be used—apparently it seemed appropriate that a vast company largely involved in a high-technology industry should avail itself of such an opportunity, however primitive!

The first day (I was scheduled to speak to four audiences) I forgot to ask any questions, but I do remember a backstage conversation immediately after I'd come off the stage. The IBM executives wanted me to remove something from my presentation. It was a mild story about a friend of mine who had been trapped in a Port-O-Let during a golf tournament while Arnold Palmer, just outside the door, was trying to concentrate on hitting a shot. It was a funny story; at worst the only off-color part of it was the mention of the Port-O-Let, but that, I suppose, in the minds of the executives, put the story in the outhouse category. The IBM people were quite apologetic about their primness, but they were also firm. The year before, O. J. Simpson had stunned them (though not necessarily the audience) with some off-color material. It had come unexpectedly as they stood offstage, looking in from the wings at the great athlete standing at midstage telling bawdy jokes, and they were unable to do anything about it.

I was somewhat startled at their reaction to my story and especially that I was being criticized. I don't know any dirty jokes or stories. My recriminatory arsenal of oaths comprises such epithets as "drat," "dad-blame," "Lordy," and "for Pete's sake." To be warned about off-color material and to have a story deleted from my presentation . . . well, it was almost heady! In any case, I agreed to remove the Port-O-Let story.

Once again I was urged to ask questions of the audience so the push-button system could be used. The next afternoon I found a place in midspeech to do so. I told my audience that James Thurber, *The New Yorker* humorist, had once suggested that 95 percent of the males in America put themselves to sleep striking out the batting order of the New York Yankees (much easier now than then, I said to raise a laugh) and that I had always wondered if this figure was accurate. Perhaps they could help me. I asked how many agreed with Mr. Thurber. The members of the audience murmured as they bent over their armrests.

I have forgotten the exact figure that flashed up on the screen behind me, except that it was a number well below the Thurber estimate.

I then gave them an alternate. How many of them put themselves to sleep at night dreaming of Bo Derek, the willowy actress whose presence in a film called *10* (in which she appeared in a white bathing suit and often less) had made a considerable impact on the public? Once again, the murmur of voices, shadowy fingers probing in the semidark for the buttons in the armrests.

When the tabulations were done, the figure suddenly flashed on the screen—69! Filling the back of the stage, the number glowed there, immutable, stunning us. A titter rose. It was evident that my audience knew the number's sexual connotation. Suddenly someone couldn't contain himself and burst into a violent guffaw. It ignited the rest—600 people, finally, pounding their knees, rocking back and forth, letting loose with such a concussion of laughter that I felt it was almost palpable, swaying as I stood on the stage in its gusts sweeping across the footlights . . . of such magnitude that it was as if all those years of putting on the white shirts and sensible ties and the blue suits and the rest were preparing one for this ironic, mighty smack at the whole system. It was as if Watson Sr. himself had appeared in his blue suit, etc., and congratulated them for being elected to the Gold Circle, and stated how proud IBM was of their contribution, and then, being a wild duck, had turned and mooned them from center stage.

Finally the laughter died away. Shaken, I thanked the

audience for its cooperation (which got them laughing again), and I went on with the talk. From time to time, irrespective of what I was saying, a murmur of laughter would start up again and die away, like the mutter of a summer storm.

In the wings after it was over, I told the IBM officials I was sorry. "It was really out of my control."

They understood. Of course they understood. They were the ones who had urged me to use the system. The executive group kept what I thought was a pretty stiff upper lip about what had happened. They didn't seem very much amused. Perhaps they were annoyed that the audience had started laughing. They seemed like teachers whose kindergarten pupils had suddenly erupted out of control.

But the next afternoon they seemed much more cheerful. "You can use the buttons," they said. "Everything's been fixed."

"What?"

"You can ask them about Bo Derek."

"I can?"

"What we've done is to program that number right out of the system!"

5

THE PRESIDENT TELEPHONED. It was about a month after his inauguration. At the time of the call I was sitting in the office of *The Paris Review* in New York. It is cramped. A bicycle hangs from hooks in the ceiling; the editors have to duck under it to sit at their desks. Sometimes four editors are crammed in under there. One of them picked up the phone and, with a startled look on his face, handed it to me. "It's the White House calling," he said. "The president." He handed me the receiver.

"Yes, Mr. President," I said.

It wasn't the president, of course, but a secretary down the line. After a while the president himself came on—his voice unmistakable and so clear that my fellow editors, leaning out of their chairs, could listen in.

"Nice to hear from you, sir," I said cheerfully.

He had called to invite me to Washington to be on hand when the horseshoe pit was inaugurated at a ribbon-cutting ceremony. Some horseshoe experts were coming in, and we'd get a chance to play again. The rematch.

I looked in my calendar and discovered I was scheduled to be in San Diego on that day.

"I can't do it, sir."

"What?"

"I've been asked to be the grand marshal of a crew regatta," I said miserably.

"Get it over with and catch the red-eye back East," the president suggested. "Rest up here at the White House. We have lots of room," he explained, as if asking a guest to a country home.

My editors nodded their heads.

I explained that my presence was required throughout the regatta, that I was expected to hand out trophies at the final ceremonies. "Yale has sent some shells," I said feebly. "They may win. . . . "

The president finally gave up trying to convince me. "Well, we'll have to postpone the rematch," he said. "We'll miss you at the ceremonies." He said he looked forward to the match when it could be arranged, and hung up.

My staff stared at me.

I shrugged my shoulders. "It gives me more time to prepare."

■ ■ ■

AT A DINNER party that night, word got around the table that the president had called.

"Trying to get you to run the country for a day?" someone gibed.

The guests looked down the length of the table. I told them that years ago President Kennedy, whom I knew and who was vaguely interested in my participatory-journal-ism stints, had done exactly that—invited me down to run the country for a day. "Then he picked the day," I said. "February 31st!"

"And what day has Bush picked?"

"Not germane," I answered. "He only wants me to play horseshoes."

Talk about preparing for the horseshoe match started up around the table. The suggestion I remember best came from someone who must have been a history major at college: "I've always heard that every great athlete was motivated by a kind of controlled rage," he said. "It's not only sports. The energy of all sorts of successful people is fueled by an anger—sometimes conscious, often not. It galvanizes. It is directed against any number of targets—authority, family, race, indignity, another's principles—and one is driven to success out of spite.

"Now, I understand you're a Democrat," he said, looking up from the other end of the table. "What you need to do is think up every indignity the Republicans have ever heaped on society over the years—in no particu-lar order, the Depression, McCarthyism, Watergate, James Watt, Crédit Mobilier, Teapot Dome, robber bar-ons, Smoot-Hawley, anti-unionism, the '87 crash . . . you let all this simmer, and then take it down to Washington and mentally level it at Bush. Controlled rage, that's what it is. Think Teapot Dome!"

"Very funny," my dinner companion had said after-ward in the taxi.

"But not very helpful."

"You're much too serious about all this," she said. "Let's go dancing somewhere," she suggested. "It'll im-prove your footwork."

■ ■ ■

THE GUEST AT dinner was certainly on to something—controlled rage was very likely a part of the X Factor. Bill Russell, the Boston Celtics star center, once told me that he would lie in his hotel room before a game and imagine that he was the sheriff in a Western cow town where a gang of black hats (the Philadelphia 76ers or the Atlanta Hawks, whatever team the Celtics were playing that night) had turned up and were running roughshod through the place, beating up people and gunning down a few. In his mind he worked up a coldblooded rage and stalked them through the dusty streets, knocking them off one by one. Athletes learn to turn on this controlled rage—some quicker than others. Bill Curry told me that before the Colts went out onto the field, Mike Curtis, the middle linebacker they called "Animal," would ask a teammate to belt him alongside the helmet, wallop him, which would ignite the rage, like a light switch clicked on.

Actually, *uncontrolled* rage tends to be more interesting to write about. I have always treasured a sight of Tommy Heinsohn, when he coached the Boston Celtics, leveling a kick at the bucket that contained oranges to suck on, missing it, and having his loafer, a very large model, sailing up into the mezzanine. In baseball, the water cooler at the end of the dugout was traditionally the target of rage, though other inanimate objects were often larger. The Chicago pitcher "Mad Monk" Meyers was sitting peacefully enough in a bathroom stall one afternoon, when suddenly rage over some indignity on the pitcher's mound swept over him; he got up and ripped the latrine door off its hinges. Hank Greenberg told me that his pitcher-teammate Fred Hutchinson used to break lightbulbs, swatting at them with his glove as he headed down the corridor that led from the Detroit Tigers dugout back to the locker room. When he later became a manager, the fungo bat became the instrument of his frustration—he would pound it on the dugout steps until it snapped. Usually three or four fungo bats, which are used for fielding practice, will last a club through the season. The Tigers would order up a dozen or so because they knew that Hutchinson would break most of them during the summer. Jim Brosnan, the ex-Cubs and Reds pitcher, who wrote a wonderful baseball book called *The Long Season*, told me this about Hutchinson: "When the Tigers lost, he was no one to live with. His wife would hear the news on the radio or watch it on television, and she'd turn and warn the children. One time Hutch came home after a Tiger loss—sometimes he walked miles along Michigan Avenue to try to cool down—and to everyone's surprise he seemed to be making an effort to keep his temper in check. He sat down for dinner with his family. He didn't say much. Then, just as he was getting up from his dessert, he turned and threw a punch in frustration, busting a hole in the wall right behind his chair. His wife cried out, 'Look, Hutch, what you've done!' and he growled, 'Hang a picture over it,' and stomped out."

Hutchinson would have felt very much at home with an Indian tribe called the Yanomamö living in southern Venezuela and northern Brazil. Described in 1988 by a sociologist named Napoleon Chagnon, its members operate socially in a constant state of rage. Indeed, a quick, fiery temper and a readiness to use violence are considered virtues in their culture. Wives, as might be expected, have a miserable time. The males not only work themselves into a rage at the slightest provocation, but seek to bring others to the boiling point with insults, face slaps, and so forth, which Chagnon describes as being close to an imitation of the power-announcing behavior of apes.

One might think this a complete reversal of the decorum required of our Western culture, where anger (except in the case, as we've seen, of the odd athlete) is kept pretty much in check, certainly in the genteel circles of big business. Not so. I have been reading Bryan Burrough and John Helyar's *Barbarians at the Gate*, an account of the largest takeover in Wall Street history—the fight to control RJR Nabisco during October and November of 1988. As I turned the pages, it struck me how often the players in the drama behaved like members of the Yanomamö. What follows is by no means a complete listing:

Weigl stormed . . . and stormed . . . and stormed.

He [Horrigan] began to cry, his fury and frustration producing tears that streamed down his cheeks in torrents.

Johnson simmered.

Kohlberg exploded.

Cy Lewis hit the roof.

Spangler stewed.

Kravis began to grow angry. "I can't believe this," he fumed.

Beck was fuming.

Tempers flared.

Kravis could barely contain his anger.

After much gnashing of teeth, Kohlberg . . .

Cohen's anger quickly gave way to shock.

"Goddamn it," Kravis fumed. "I've never been so mad in my life!"

Ted Forstmann had been angry for five years now.

Jim Robinson silently cursed cellular phones.

Slowly, a stream of profanity, like some earthy ticker

tape, began scrolling through Forstmann's mind.

Cohen was pacing about, uttering foul things about Kravis.

Boisi stormed out.

Kravis exploded.

Hill bridled.

Strauss was too much of a gentleman to curse Kravis that morning.

Bagley strode around his lawyer's office, waving his arms and violating the dignified hush of Arnold & Porter's Washington office.

Cohen was still fuming.

Forstmann was so mad he felt the blood drain from his face.

Raether was in a foul mood.

Hostility radiated from the man [Kravis] like summer heat from a city street.

Goldstone stormed around the corner into Johnson's office. Spitting mad . . .

He [Kravis] was livid . . . "pissing fire."

Johnson simmered in his office.

For the first time in a month Johnson lost his temper.

Kravis, raising his voice, said, "I'm going to break both your kneecaps!"

"There's a rat fink in the room," Hugel said.

Colleagues remember Maher stomping out of Wasserstein's office from time to time shouting "You asshole!" at the top of his lungs.

Maher exploded.

"This is shit!" Fennebresque ranted behind closed doors.

Maher exploded, kicking the leg of his mahogany desk and slamming his fists violently onto the top.

Ed Horrigan was nearly foaming at the mouth.

Goldstone was on the verge of hysteria.

Horrigan was in a white fury.

As they [Kravis's troops] rode down to the lobby, the elevator was filled with curses and shouts.

Beattie was incensed. "We've been screwed!"

"We've been robbed!" Martin yelled. "We've been robbed!"

Shouts of anguish erupted within the Range Rover.

Gordon Rich lost it. He grabbed his gray plastic phone, stretched the cord to its full length and hurled the receiver against the console with all his strength.

Monday found Johnson in a foul mood.

In no time Horrigan was raging at the board, at Kravis, at everything.

"This is bullshit!" Gutfreund railed.

Roberts hit the roof.

Curses filled the room.

Nusbaum nearly choked.

When Roberts was mad, his lips became small and tight, slits in an angry face.

Roberts was so angry he followed the two members into the bathroom. . . .

Charlie Hugel's gout flared up.

With every bit of anger he [Roberts] tore into Lovejoy.

Horrigan grew bitter and morose.

Fuming, Kravis and Roberts sat back to wait.

"You're [Martin] the most ineffective, immature son of a bitch that ever walked the face of the earth!" Horrigan shouted.

Enough! Somewhere in *Barbarians at the Gate* is this somewhat wistful sentence: "During the '50s, Reynolds was one great, happy family."

■　■　■

I WENT TO see one of these angry men—Henry Kravis himself, who had engineered the $25 billion takeover of the RJR Nabisco company. He agreed to speak with me about the X Factor. The reception room of Kohlberg, Kravis, Roberts (KKR) is on the forty-second floor of the Avon Building. The windows look out on Central Park. It was afternoon and the day was extremely clear; I could see north to the Connecticut horizon. The park itself seemed like a private enclave. The X Factor, it occurred to me, could very well be engendered by the view from the windows of KKR: it would be hard to sit at a desk, as Henry Kravis does every day, and look out the window and not feel that the world was one's oyster . . . that at eleven o'clock, if so wished, one could take the elevator down to the stables and change to ride out to the hounds of the Central Park Hunt. The image of English country-house glamour was enhanced by the muted elegance of the reception room—Stubbs-school paintings of horses hanging on paneled walls, rich carpets on parquet floors. The receptionist sat at a massive desk trimmed in brass with a green leather top. I inspected a painting called *Union Scout*, which showed a group of mounted soldiers emerging from a wood. They are startled, the horses rearing; in the distance the white streak of a lightning bolt is striking a tree. I wondered vaguely if this was symbolic—that the tree was a company involved in a hostile takeover.

Henry Kravis appeared. He was wearing a white collar over a light pink shirt. Slim, elegant, he seemed most collected and not at all like someone from whom anger could rise like summer heat from a city street. Or who would suggest breaking someone's kneecaps. We walked through a series of doors that sprung open at the touch of a button—a kind of security procedure. What could they be guarding? I wondered. Surely not the proceeds to finance these enormous deals. Lives, probably. We reached Kravis's office, a smaller and more personalized version of the reception room—family photographs on bookshelves and his desk. We stood at the windows. He pointed out Leona Helmsley's penthouse at the top of the Park Lane Hotel. At the south end is a glassed-in extension that probably contained a large garden shed or small swimming pool—Kravis wasn't sure which. For financial misdeeds, she was facing jail and a somewhat limited view compared to what she has from the Park Lane Hotel. It was an odd, disquieting sight in that extraordinary view from Kravis's office—perhaps a reminder that things could go very wrong in the world of high finance.

At one end of his office was a sofa and comfortable chairs covered with bright chintz. We sat down. "I've been reading *Barbarians at the Gate*," I said. "Why do all you people in there seem so angry?"

He smiled. "Well," he said, "you'll remember the stakes were very high. People who believe in what they're doing—whether it's writing a book or playing a game—become passionate . . . wrapped up in it. You're in competition. A lot of dumb things were done . . . leaks to the press . . . and certainly that created some of the anger."

I asked if fear, the instilling of it, was a useful ingredient in his line of work.

He shook his head. "Fear of being fired? No, you can't run a company by ranting and raving, because at some point people lose respect for you. Beyond that, because it's a one-man dictatorship, they don't feel they have any role."

I wondered if a kind of X Factor was involved. Was there an overriding principle that guided the workings of KKR?

"Absolutely," Kravis said. "I've always said to the people at the firm that if you don't play your position, then the team doesn't move forward. I don't ever want to hear at KKR 'that's my idea' or 'I did this' or 'I did that.' I want it to be 'we did this.' We're small enough—we have only sixteen professionals—so that George Roberts and I know what everybody's doing. People are 'incentivized' in such a way that they really are pulling for the team, and that's everyone at KKR—from the receptionist at the front door, to the ladies who serve the lunches, to the secretaries, to the senior partners. We are owners in our companies—as opposed to paying everyone a salary, a bonus, and with only two people or so at the top owning all the equity. We think that if the lady at the front desk has an ownership position in every company we buy, she's going to care a little more."

"You mean that secretary out there by the elevator?" I asked incredulously.

"Well, she doesn't put any money in," Kravis said, "but she gets options vested over a period of time. We incentivize her in a different way. We want her to stay here. Down the road we can give her a big check when we sell one of these companies or they go public. But for those in the higher echelons, who are involved in a transaction, what's very important is that they put their money where their mouth is—so they have something at risk.

"One of the problems I see in corporations in this country," Kravis continued, "is that managements today are 'renters' of the corporate assets—they're not owners anymore. The day of the Carnegies, the Mellons, the Rockefellers—they're over. What happened was that over the generations the families brought in professional managers; the ownership was dissipated. U.S. Steel was started and built by a family, and then the renters come in with their objective to see how big they can make the company—not how profitable, but how big—and all along living off the assets: the jet airplanes, the golf courses, and so on. The X Factor here with us is that we're owners; we think like owners. When you're an owner you start asking questions that maybe you wouldn't ask otherwise." He shifted in his chair. "Psychologically, it's as though you have a brand-new Mercedes. You polish it, you're not going to want any dents in it, and so forth. Then you make a trip. You go to Avis and rent a nice car. You get a little scratch on the side; you're not very happy about it, but so what. It's not your car. You turn it back in, and you're off to the next thing—there's no real damage to you. So what I call X Factor in business is that you think like an owner."

I asked, "Well, what about the process of becoming an owner?"

"Well, of course you have to get there," Kravis agreed. "I've always been a believer in the concept 'don't tell me you can't do it.' I tell my children the word 'can't' is not in their vocabulary; just take it out. Some things, of course, you legitimately cannot do, but it's an attitude you should cultivate. I've always had the attitude that I could fall out this window, bounce on my head a couple of times, figuratively, and make myself come up on my feet."

Forty-two floors, I thought.

"I love competition," he was saying. "I thrive on it. I learned it as a young man. I wrestled. When I was in the seventh and eighth grades in Tulsa, Oklahoma, these magazine companies would come around to the school and get the kids out on these magazine drives, contests to see who could sell the most. I just loved that. I'd collect old newspapers in my wagon and stack them in the garage, and then I'd load them up in the trunk of the car. My mother would drive me over to the newspaper recycling plant and I'd get six cents a pound, or whatever, for these old newspapers. Each time I tried to do better than I'd done the time before."

I asked, "Well, what was the motivation for this? Was it the money?"

"Oh, no. Not at all," Kravis said. "The competition . . . just not wanting to lose."

"Is it all a game?" I asked. "Was the RJR takeover a contest in that sense?"

"No," he said. "Careers and people's livelihoods were involved. Gamesmanship, perhaps. Letting people believe you're not going to bid. RJR was clearly not a game, because there was too much at stake. But it was a challenge, and I have always liked challenges. People ask, 'Why do you keep working so hard? You've already made a lot of money, you don't need to work.' I say, 'It's pretty simple. It's not the money—clearly not that. If I'm going to compete, then I want to win, and in a moral, ethical framework.' "

"When you talk about a moral, ethical framework, what about the by-products of buyouts—golden parachutes and such things?"

"I am disturbed by them," Kravis replied. "People are often rewarded for doing a lousy job. The incentive is in the wrong place. It's a 'heads I win, tails you lose' scenario. If I don't do a good job and somebody takes me over, then fine; I've still got my golden parachute and I'm gone. That's wrong. The executive should be on the same side of the table as the shareholders. Unfortunately, that is not often the case. I'm against golden parachutes, except to a certain degree and in certain circumstances. For example, a fellow may have done a very good job for a company, but for some reason the stock is trading at a low price, no fault of management at all, and along comes a raider and throws his people out. In that instance I can understand a golden parachute. What I don't sympathize with is when people have done a mediocre job and walk away with millions of dollars at shareholders' expense."

"Do you think the government should step in?" I asked. "Should golden parachutes be legislated against?"

"Well, the government has to a certain extent," Kravis said. "Taxes now make it very difficult to have the same kind of golden parachute one used to have."

He paused and his voice changed slightly, as if he imagined himself speaking to a larger audience. "I wish there was a way to do this," he said. "I'd like to see that the boards of directors of public companies are major owners of these companies . . . and in relation to their net worth. A teacher on the board, or a college president, or a doctor can't afford a lot of stock, but there are a lot of people who can afford it. Nor should directors sit on fifteen different boards. They should be on perhaps three boards and have a real portion of their net worth at risk. I guarantee you in that case they'd hold management accountable. Right now, no one is holding management accountable. Institutional investors own about 60 to 70 percent of most big company stocks today. If the institution's unhappy, they can call the president, but they'll be lucky to get a return phone call. Or its people will be told, 'If you're not happy, sell your stock.' That's about all that can happen. An institution like the Prudential Insurance Company is not going to start a tender offer takeover fund or a proxy fight to throw the management out. So, until somebody holds them accountable, a lot of managements are not going to change. A big problem is that too many boards work on the principle that 'you be on my board, I'll be on your board; we'll be buddies and play golf every week and live across the street from each other, and I won't ask too many questions and you won't ask too many questions on our respective boards, and life will go on.' "

I shifted in my chair and told Kravis that I had always been fascinated by what went through the minds of professional athletes, especially in the moments of stress just before a game. Could he talk about his thought processes as a businessman?

"Well, obviously a lot runs through my mind," he said. "Let's say I'm thinking of buying an RJR Nabisco. I think what could be done with this company, where we could make it more productive, how we could make it grow and make our return on investment more profitable. That's continually going through my mind. We have analysts and consultants come in. Also going on in my mind would be the financing, the right capital structure, how much equity and how much debt should be in place so that the company has flexibility to grow, to move into different areas. Then I think about what happens if the market turns down. I ask myself where the downside is in this investment; how low can the earnings or the cash flow go, given the capital structure? Will the company still be on safe ground? Very important. If I have my downside protected, pretty typically I'll make money all the time. In fact, I worry more about my downside than the upside. At the same time I'm thinking about RJR Nabisco, I'm also concerned with our portfolio companies—more than thirty-five different companies we've bought since 1976, which we've spent about $68 billion buying. I'm thinking how they're doing. Are they meeting our expectations? Where can we improve them? What should we do to take the risk out of a particular company by changing the capital structure? I'm also thinking about whether we have the right management in the various companies. I do a lot of thinking very early in the morning. My wife, Carolyne, always kids me because I'll be lying in bed with my hands behind my head. She'll say, 'You're in your thinking position, aren't you?' It's about the only time I do have. During the day I'm lucky to have time to really think, because it's one meeting after another or telephone calls or whatever, group discussions, batting ideas around."

"To get back to the X Factor," I asked, "which in your case seems to have a lot to do with competitiveness. Is that ever a problem?"

"It is a danger," Kravis said quickly. "It has to be controlled. Earlier in my life I'd get carried away with a product. For example, I like to fish. The Shakespeare Company was for sale—they make fishing rods. I did everything to figure out how to buy the company, and I could never make the numbers work right. Finally, one of my partners came to me and said, 'Would you just give up on this company? It's not going to work. I'll buy you a new fishing rod and a new reel and you'll be happy.' It was an interesting lesson to me, because you do have to look at these things objectively. Mistakes are made a lot of times when one gets too emotionally involved. You can believe in a product, but don't get married to it: things are always changing; you've got to be flexible. All too often people say, 'I've just got to own a baseball team. I don't care what I pay for it.' Fortunately, most baseball owners can afford it, so it doesn't make any difference. But God forbid if he can't. He's made the wrong decision because he's not being objective. That's what happened to Robert Campeau, the Canadian entrepreneur. Mr. Campeau wanted to be the biggest retailer in the world. His ego got in the way, just totally in the way. It wasn't even a matter of being competitive. He wanted to be the biggest retailer; that was the way it was going to be. There was plenty of financing around so he got to be the biggest retailer. Look what's happened to him. A couple of his businesses are bankrupt."

"One would have thought his advisers would have stepped in or at least warned him."

Kravis nodded. "It's very important to have advisers around to bounce ideas off of—to have people you totally trust. I'm not afraid to be told that I'm wrong or that I'm off base. I want smart people around me. The smarter the better. A lot of people make very big mistakes because they have yes-men around, because they don't want to be shown up."

"Do you think one is born with your kind of competitiveness?" I asked.

He nodded and said that much of it had to have come from his parents. "My father was in the oil-and-gas business . . . full of risks. He lost all his money in the Depression, got back on his feet, and made a huge success of himself. Independence was the best lesson my parents ever taught me—be on your own. My mother tells me that when I was a little boy she'd come into the room to tie my shoes and help me get dressed, and I'd say, 'No, it's me myself,' meaning 'I'll tie it myself.' "

"Do you think independence can be learned?" I asked.

"I would guess the X Factor is something instilled in you," he replied, "and then it's fostered."

I told him that I was going to play horseshoes with the president. Did he have any suggestions? How would he prepare if he were in my place?

He laughed. "Damned if I know," he said. "I suppose I'd go up to my house in the country, put two stakes in, and throw horseshoes at them. Practice a little bit. That's all I'd do. After all, it's the president's sport. Have some fun and get it over with."

He glanced briefly at his watch. "I have dreams every once in a while," he said reflectively. "The dream is that I'm back in school and I can't find my classroom. It's final-exam time. I'm nervous as can be, and I wake up in a cold sweat. Apparently it's a very common anxiety dream for people who set high goals for themselves. It comes out of a combination of anxiety and frustration, because you set these high goals you may not be able to achieve. My father, who's now about eighty-eight, still has those dreams."

He looked at me questioningly. "Do you have dreams like that?"

"Yes, many times," I said. "But my dreams are a little different, and worse. What happens to me is that I find the classroom where the exam is being given. I sit down, open the blue book, and I haven't got the slightest idea what the questions are about. In fact, the thought crosses my mind that I'm in the wrong class." I paused. Kravis was grinning. "That's not quite the same as yours, is it?" I said. "I suspect that if you ever found the classroom in your dream you'd sit down, open up the blue book, answer the questions, and get an A."

He smiled and shrugged.

I couldn't resist. "Mr. Kravis," I said. "I'm the editor of *The Paris Review*. Are you interested in the takeover, a very friendly one, of a small literary magazine?"

"No," he said cheerfully. "Absolutely not."

■ ■ ■

NOT LONG AFTER, I found myself chatting with Michael Thomas, who writes a lively, usually acerbic column, mostly on financial matters, for the New York *Observer*. He has a Wall Street background, having served a stint at Lehmann Bros.

"So you've been talking to Kravis," he said. "A lot of the merger and acquisition people are failed marines," he went on. "Too young for one war, too old for the next. In *Barbarians at the Gate* Kravis says at one point: 'We'll come up out of the rice paddies with all guns firing.' So you've got this combination of the military with the athletic. For them it's all a game—a giant Monopoly game. Or mud-wrestling. Take your pick. Since they don't know anything about the companies they're competing for, they're driven by ego, greed, rage. The people who are going to win are the ones who want it more. How many times have we heard that hoary locker-room cliché?"

I asked if he thought these competitors thought of themselves as sportsmen.

"Perhaps not sportsmen but certainly players," Michael said. "I'm sure Sir James Goldsmith thinks of his merger and acquisitions activities in England as a game."

I said I had known Goldsmith years ago in Paris and doubted that he had ever picked up a cricket bat or kicked a ball.

"Gambling," Michael replied. "He learned his competitiveness fleecing some second-rate Arab at the gaming tables in Deauville. Now he gets his excitement banco-ing a billion-dollar industry. It's a high-stakes game."

He reminded me of the scene in Michael Lewis's best-seller *Liar's Poker* in which John Gutfreund, the head of Salomon Bros., challenges a bond trader named Meriwether to play one hand of liar's poker for a million dollars, and Meriwether counters in the best gambling-saloon tradition by agreeing to play for *ten* million—an offer Gutfreund somewhat ruefully backs away from.

Michael urged me to look through *Barbarians at the Gate* to pick up the sports comparisons. "They jump off the page," he said. "An easy merger—they call it a 'slam dunk.'"

He went on to describe Ross Johnson, the CEO of Nabisco, and his obsession with sports figures: his company spent over $10 million annually on what was called Team Nabisco. Its members included Jack Nicklaus, Alex Webster, Bobby Orr, Don Meredith, Ron Laver, Fuzzy Zoeller. Meredith got a half million a year. Frank Gifford received over $400,000 along with a New York apartment and an office. The king of the roost was Jack Nicklaus, who got a million dollars annually and was rather begrudging about it, refusing to appear for Nabisco functions more than five or six times a year. Reggie Jackson of the New York Yankees, a Johnson pal, had a candy bar named after him which Nabisco produced—the *Reggie!* it was called—a chocolate-and-peanut concoction handed out to fans entering Yankee Stadium, and which failed within the year.

"I'll tell you something about all these takeover guys," Michael said. "They're small—watch-charm players. All the players in the Nabisco takeover are little people. Peter Cohen at Shearson is five-six; Eric Gleacher at Morgans is five-eight; Henry Kravis is five-six."

I mentioned that my friend Gene Scott had made the

same observations about the domination of tennis by small-statured players. "What's a watch-charm player?" I asked.

"Remember those small feisty guards who gritted it up and got on Walter Camp's All American squad? You'd have these big guys on the line, 240, 245, 230, and then sandwiched in there among them would be a 180-pounder . . . a watch-charm player, small enough to fit on your watch-chain."

We started trading tycoons, like cards.

I offered Martin Sorell, the advertising mogul just a few inches over five feet, who bought out J. Walter Thompson for a billion.

"Si Newhouse, five-two. Saul Steinberg, five-four."

I forgot at the time, but I should have remembered Allen H. Newhart, the CEO of Gannett Publications. A small man himself (five-two), he was said to have put together an executive staff of people as short or preferably shorter than he was. The joke at Gannet was that no one over five feet six inches could get very far in the organization. I could have thrown a whole blockbuster of diminutive people at Michael if I'd known their names! I met Newhart once at a party in his house in Melbourne, Florida. Someone tapped me on the shoulder. I turned around and no one was there. "I'm down here," a voice said.

6

I

HE PRESIDENT HAS been playing golf at Kennebunkport. The papers are full of it. His game is unique—speed being an important consideration. In fact, the score seems less important to him than the time it takes to get around the course; the local pro refers to a Bush round of golf as "cart polo."

I read that the president has found some new motivational phrases to go along with his game. One of them is "Mr. Smooth." "All right, now, Mr. Smooth," he murmurs to himself as he stands over the ball.

Golf has been traditionally the politicians' game (Eisenhower, Kennedy, Ford, Tip O'Neill, Quayle, et al.) but also the CEO's favorite outdoor pastime. It provides a kind of microcosm of corporate life without any of the complexities—challenges (the course), options and decisions (which club to use), financial involvement ($5 Nassaus), competition (playing partners), success (the sinking of a long putt), and failure (the duck hook)—all of this played out in a spirit of camaraderie over a summer day in an environment rich with the accoutrements of success: beautifully groomed and landscaped fairways and greens; the country club with its oak-lined taproom; the locker room with its carpet soft to the feet on the way to the shower; a shoe-shine attendant whose first name is known to everyone and his last to nobody. Best of all, the institution is totally permanent. One can play in it far beyond retirement years; there is a handicap system that puts one, whatever age, on par with the immortals.

The CEO's real-life ultimate in golf (besides being asked to play hurry-up golf at Kennebunkport) is to be invited to play in the AT&T Pebble Beach National Pro-Am Tournament. Not only do the CEOs enjoy the privilege of hobnobbing with the more powerful of their kind, along with screen and sports stars, but they have the chance to appear on national television with the pros as their partners. There can hardly be a CEO in the country who does not recall James D. Robinson III, the CEO of American Express, known familiarly as "Jimmy Three-Sticks" from those Roman numerals, calmly chipping a shot over a trap and into the hole of the 18th at Del Monte—on national television, what's more! This was probably CEOism at its most glorious, with hardly an executive in the country not leaning out of his armchair to catch it: "Look at ol' Three-Sticks, that son of a bitch!"— half in envy, half in admiration.

Recently, I called up Robinson to talk about it. I got through to him largely, I think, because I told his secretary I wanted to ask him about "the shot."

"Tom Kite was my partner," Robinson said. "We came up to the 18th—the final group, huge crowd circling the green, national television—and I found that I was looking at a delicate chip shot over a sand trap. *Well*, I thought, *there's a good chance I'll knock the ball into the trap, or worse, skull it over the green and hit someone in the crowd. It'll be the end of me.* I thought about picking up. Tom was about to win the tournament, but we weren't going to win the team event. Instead, I turned to my caddie and I said, 'Let me have the sand wedge, because I'm going to sink it.' And I did!"

"Like a dream," I commented. "You were in the zone."

"To this day it's the single most important thing I've done in my life."

I blinked and asked if perhaps being the chairman of American Express wasn't comparable.

"Oh, no," Robinson said. "I can clearly tell by the acclaim I get traveling around the world. People come up and they say, 'I saw that shot!' They don't say, 'I recall the day you became chairman.' That year I went up to Albany with the New York City Partnership [a business lobbying group], which we do every year, to meet with the Senate leadership. Before that shot I always had to stand in line and introduce myself. This time, Warren Anderson, the majority leader, came right over to me, with David Rockefeller and a lot of others waiting, and he said, 'That was the most impressive shot I have ever seen!' He then proceeded at some length to tell me about a shot *he'd* made while playing with Bob Hope. From then on we were bosom buddies.

"There's a whole practical side to sports," Robinson went on. "In a sports environment you get to know something about people, how they come across, how they manage their emotions. . . . "

I asked, "Would you have trouble promoting someone who . . . well, suddenly snapped a putter across his knee after missing a shot?"

Robinson demurred and said he didn't take people out on the golf course to promote or fire them. "Periodically I'll take some of our management down to the Augusta National or out to Cypress Point," he said, "because those are legendary courses. So (a) they really appreciate it, and (b) it gets us off for a couple of days so we can get to know one another in an environment other than behind a desk or in the conference room. They do the same sort of thing with *their* customers. It's an appropriate part of a total process."

I asked what his golf handicap was. An 8. Physical fitness is a big thing with him. Every morning he does from 600 to 1,000 sit-ups. He has all the machines. American Express has a physical-fitness program called "Wellness."

"Good Lord," I said. "How long does it take to do 600 to 1,000 sit-ups?"

"Twenty minutes to a half-hour. It sets an example. It's important to have a fit and determined work force."

He got talking about conducting management affairs, that they should be handled in the manner of a "benevolent Lombardi" (a nice oxymoron) and that the focus should be to create a team that would, as he put it, "win Super Bowls every day, not simply annually."

When he gets talking about his company, he goes on this way—I was told afterward—with little snippets he recalls from speeches exhorting his troops: "The will to win is part of the fiber of this country." "A determination to win is vital in the business context." "You've got to have a core set of values . . . march to the quality drum-beat." "I have often said," he told me, "that I want on my tombstone the word *quality*."

"I beg your pardon?"

"Quality. That's the one thing since 1975 that I've focused on most at American Express."

Afterward, I wondered about "quality" on one's tombstone. Someone wandering through the cemetery, not knowing it was a company catchword, might assume Robinson wished to have it descriptive of *himself*, which, while doubtless true, might seem . . . well, a bit cocky. Some other less self-serving possibilities came to mind. Why not something to commemorate his great shot at Del Monte on the 18th? "The Chipper," with his dates underneath. Or at the very least, if the American Express association was to be identified, why not the famous slogan "Don't leave home without it"? Or surely more intriguing: "I left home without it."

■ ■ ■

"DOES THE POPE play golf?"

I was on the phone with Michael Novak, a distinguished theologian whose book *The Joy of Sports* is perhaps the best treatise on the impact of sport on society. Novak is a passionate fan. After a bad day, his spirits are lifted simply by the knowledge that on television that night he'll be able to watch the Dodgers in Montreal.

At one point he had written, "I have never met a person who disliked sports, or who absented himself or herself entirely from them, who did not seem to me deficient in humanity . . . such persons seem to me a danger to civilization."

I had reached Novak to ask him about this. He agreed

that perhaps he had put it a bit strongly. "I do feel, though," he said, "a firm spiritual ground with people who have been involved with sport. Unless you've gone through that particular kind of struggle involved in sport . . . there's a certain lack. Sport teaches you how difficult things are."

That was when I asked about the pope and golf. "Does the pope . . . I mean, what sort of background does the pope have in sports?"

"He's an excellent skier."

"Oh?"

"He was a soccer goalie. I don't know about golf."

The thought of the pope sailing down a mountain with his clerical robes billowing out behind settled for an instant in my mind.

Novak was saying that he had been rereading Tocqueville, about the way Americans approached commerce, contrasting it with the Europeans. The main difference is that Americans approach everything with the zeal of the revolutionary; they delight in chance and risk . . . a pervasive element all across America.

"Sports—baseball first—celebrates this, and very powerfully."

"Why baseball?" I asked.

Novak replied that baseball had powers even he hadn't suspected. He had asked a South Korean businessman to explain the economic recovery and development of a country broken by war.

"What the Korean said was that they had studied the Japanese very carefully and discovered two secrets. In order to develop, a country needs either chopsticks or calligraphy, preferably both, *and* to play baseball. I had laughed, and the Korean had said, 'No, no, I'm serious.

Look at China. They use chopsticks, but they don't play baseball. Look at Cuba. They play baseball, but they don't use chopsticks.'

"And then he explained. Chopsticks teach a fine coordination between the brain and the hand—crucial, since the finest quality in manufacturing is going to win in the marketplace. Secondly, Asians have always been collectivists—the Confucian idea of family, community, ancestor worship, and all that—and the result is that they have no theory of the individual. He said that baseball teaches them that. Baseball singles you out. The lone player approaches the plate. The ball moves toward a single player who must deal with it."

Novak went on to say that baseball offers the best characterizations of John Locke, of the Constitution. "The framers were trying to build an association in which the individual would play a larger role than ever before. Baseball is a magnificent celebration of that."

"So individualism is the key?"

"Well, it doesn't quite work out that way in the real world. We have evolved more toward football," Novak replied. "The first thing you have to do starting a business is hire a lawyer. Second, you have to work with suppliers. Customers. Teamwork! That's probably more appropriate. I tried to explain this once to a cardinal at the Vatican, where everyone thinks that American business is all rugged individualism. I asked the cardinal to try to imagine what it must be like to be president of a huge company like General Electric, with almost a hundred affiliates, each with its own manager. There are only four or five hotels in the country with sufficient accommodations for all these managers (and their wives) to meet. I asked the cardinal to try to imagine what it's like for a CEO to take someone's word over the telephone when he sees him only four times a year, yet on whom he must count . . . and the degree of trust and camaraderie that has to be developed. It's not *quite* like a football team; it's never that intimate. But if you don't have the essence of teamwork, things will start to go bad—and quick. Still, football is close to the image of corporate life. Committee, committee, committee—just like huddles. Working things out. Strategy sessions. Progress is slow, careful. The love of surprise, ambush, initiative, enterprise—Tocqueville saw all of this as unique elements of the American character long before the invention of the game."

I wondered if sports as a metaphor wasn't often too simple.

"Oh, life is much more complicated," Novak said. "Sports doesn't offer any guidance in how to get along with women. Our sports were really developed for men, so they pretty much exclude half the human race. Sports by no means teaches you everything, but it is the best field for teaching fundamental ethics. For example, one lesson that's so crucial in sports is that you learn about losing. Learning how to accept a loss is a supreme test—not the winning but the losing."

Novak told me about a German professor, Eugene Rosenstock-Huessy, teaching ethics at Harvard who found that his references to European history, its great figures, did not make the same impression on students that they had in his home country. He slowly discovered that for every key point he wanted to make he could find a parallel in the sports Americans played.

"He began studying baseball, football, and so on," Novak said, "and found that he could go far by teaching the basic insights of ethics through lessons learned in playing sports—discipline, excellence, failure, spirit, suffering, seizing the moment. He found that play constituted not an interlude for Americans but a foundation of their intellectual and cultural lives."

"Either go to Harvard or play baseball."

"Something like that," the theologian said.

■　■　■

A FEW DAYS after my heady talk with Novak I sat down with Billie Jean King to talk about the X Factor. I had once played her in an exhibition in the New York Coliseum. The court was makeshift—a carpet laid down and mesh netting to keep the balls from flying out into the display area among the sporting-goods exhibits. It was all over very quickly. General Samsonov and Captain Edward J. Smith of the *Titanic* put in an early appearance. Since the match was an exhibition, and presumably to entertain the crowd grouped behind the netting, I assumed King would keep the ball in play. Not at all. She bore in behind a big serve. My desperation lobs banged against the ceiling.

She had no particular need to call upon an X Factor that day. We became friends; she was certainly someone to check with about winning characteristics.

First, I asked her about Novak's comment that sports in America, especially team sports, had neglected women.

She agreed, though she felt that schools and colleges were doing something to alleviate the problem. "The team sports *are* more important," she said. "Individual sports like golf or tennis teach you to be on your own—courage, independence, endurance, dealing with pressure. But the team sports teach 'people skills,' management know-how. They provide a training ground for so much," she said. "Cooperation, communication, working toward an objective. Body and mind working as one."

"What's the best part of it?" I asked.

"I love the challenge, the opportunity to do my best at a critical moment. I think that's the way champions feel," she said. "When the opponent is serving, a lot of people say, 'Please, God, make it a double-fault.' But for me, I *want* it. Don't you?"

I winced and admitted that I was in the less confident school. "No, I pray the other guy's serve is going into the net. Indeed, I try to *will* the ball into the net." I told her that I spent so much kinetic energy trying to will a double-fault that I had very little left over to deal with the ball when it came *over* the net.

King grinned and said, "Yes, Charlie Brown. Well, that's not to say that champions never think like that. But generally they say, 'Give me the ball. I want the opportunity.' That's the X Factor at work. Champions relish the moment. It's *f-u-u-u-n-n*"—drawing out the word as if to relish it—"when it's close. I used to dream about moments like that when I was very young, and I think how lucky I have been to be able to actually experience them."

Had she ever purposefully eased up in a match so she could get to that pressure point that gave her so much pleasure?

"I've been accused of that," King said. "I hope not, though subconsciously that may be so. The subconscious is so strong."

I told her about my horseshoe match with the president and that I would be playing him again. Did she have any suggestions? How would she prepare mentally?

"I read a lot of psychology books. I get buzzwords from them."

I asked for an example.

" 'Exaggerating' is one," she said. "If a match gets close, I slow down my rituals. If I bounce the ball twice before serving, I'll bounce it slowly, or repeat the ritual, bouncing it four times, *exaggerating*. I make absolutely sure that I have total clarity, acuteness, focus. I try to visualize (another buzzword) where I'm going to hit my serve. That's what President Bush was probably doing when he said 'remember Iowa'—visualizing a ringer, the horseshoe going through the air on a certain trajectory and landing around the stake. It's all an exercise in total commitment—technical and visual. I go through all this before I start. Then I feel the adrenaline flowing, and I know the moment has come: *Go!* and I commit myself. You're totally involved in the moment. That's what good concentration is."

I said that with all these things going on in her mind, it was hard to imagine that she could toss up the ball.

"No, no," she said. "All of this is before the commitment. Too much thinking and you're going to jam the computer."

I said I was reminded of Tim McCarver's remark. The former catcher and now baseball commentator had said about similar circumstances: "the mind is a great thing as long as you don't have to use it."

"That's it." She wished me luck in the horseshoe match. "Get yourself some nice buzzwords," she said.

■　■　■

WHEN THE X Factor really kicks in, the athlete enters a rare and blessed state known as being "in the zone"—a time span during which it seems one can do no wrong. Billie Jean King had described it to me: "Oh yes, that's when the ball looks huge and slow as it comes toward you. Those are your good days. On the bad days the ball is quick and looks like an aspirin tablet."

There is no patented entry to the zone. Athletes speak of it in awe. Lawrence Shainberg, in an article in the *New York Times Magazine*, mentions Pelé, the great Brazilian soccer player, describing the zone as a near mystical state: " . . . a strange calm . . . it was a type of euphoria; I felt I could run all day without tiring, that I could dribble through any of their team or all of them, that I could almost pass through them physically. I felt I could not be hurt. It was a very strange feeling and one I had not felt before. Perhaps it was merely confidence; but I have felt confident many times without that strange feeling of invincibility."

Shainberg goes on in his article to describe the attempts of an applied sports psychologist named Keith Henschen to train an extraordinarily talented twelve-year-old archer and Olympic prospect to get herself into the zone. Many of the exercises he gave her seemed directed at "blanking" the mind so that the unconscious would take over the shooting for her. If the conscious mind is involved, the archer worries about the score and will try to make the arrows go into the target instead of *letting* them go in.

Arnold Palmer has talked about this—"in the zone" meaning having a sense of detachment and being in another world. He compares it to what a musician must feel in the middle of a great performance: not a dreamlike state, but a kind of reverie, in which the focus is not on the present but on the opportunities ahead.

There are two famous remarks relevant to the subject—Yogi Berra's "How can I think and bat at the same time?" and O. J. Simpson's "If you take time to think, you get caught from behind."

I have a Buddhist-scholar friend, the novelist Peter Matthiessen, who is trying to help me learn to empty my mind to facilitate drifting into the zone, obviously the preferable state for the horseshoe rematch. He has a *zendo*, a meditation place, on his property on Long Island. It was once a stable. There are prayer mats on the floor. He gets me painfully into the lotus position facing a blank wall. He suggests an hour's meditation. As a mental exercise to empty the mind, he recommends that I visualize the faint turbulence left deep in the sea after a submarine has long passed. He leaves me alone. I try. I can hear the hum of bees in the honeysuckle outside the stable window. I try to block everything out. I think of the submarine's wake. It seems to work! I can feel my mind emptying, as if a plug has been pulled out of the bottom of a cistern. But then in my mind's eye a small fish swims by. I watch the flutter of its fins. Then, far beyond the fish, huge in the darkness, I spot the submarine. A port opens and from a cloud of bubbles a torpedo emerges. I can hear the whine of the propeller. I move along in its wake, sleek, like a sea otter. I pause, treading water, and watch it slam up against the side of a freighter. *Boom*! Inside the freighter the captain is in his stateroom shaving. He has an old-fashioned shaving brush. His chin is thickly lathered. He calls out, "Did you hear anything?" The floor tilts slightly under him. A woman appears in the door. She is carrying a small pistol. She asks, "Where's my cat?"

I unwind from the lotus position and stand up. My mind seethes. My legs ache. My friend is facing the wall, meditating. I decide not to tell him about the submarine, the torpedo, and the rest of it. He will accuse me of not trying. I tiptoe out.

■ ■ ■

THE RUSSIANS CALL being in the zone "the white moment." There are other terms for this phenomenon: in Japan, *ki*; in China, *ch'i*; in India, *prana*; in Tibet, *lung-gom*. To pick just one of these, the ultimate stage of *ki* is to achieve an extraordinary unity of mind and body in which athletes, or anyone for that matter (the woman who in a burst of frantic energy lifts a car to get her child out from underneath), can perform feats that astonish everyone, often themselves. The state seems to be beyond what can be achieved with conscious efforts such as mind tricks, willpower, determination, and practice. Sometimes the white moment has astonishing extensions. Examples would be Joe DiMaggio's 56-game hitting streak in 1941; Bob Gibson's pitching performance for the Cardinals in 1968, when his earned run average was 1.12—a record in modern baseball history that, like DiMaggio's, will surely never be surpassed; or, more recently, Orel Hershiser's string of 59 scoreless innings in 1988. All these feats, even to a statistician, surpass the laws of probability to an extent that suggests a level has been reached at which skill is not the only determinant. In other sports, golfer Byron Nelson's string of 11 straight PGA victories in 1945 would compare. Wilt Chamberlain's 100 points scored in an NBA game on March 2, 1962, against the New York Knicks in Hershey, Pennsylvania, certainly applies; so would Los Angeles Rams quarterback Norm Van Brocklin's 554-yard passing game against the New York Yanks on September 28, 1951; Walter Payton's 275-yard rushing game against Minnesota on November 20, 1977; Tom Dempsey's 63-yard field goal on November 8, 1970. I remember Alex Karras, the Detroit defensive tackle, telling me that his teammates were laughing as they saw the New Orleans Saints lining up for this field-goal attempt. The kick was three yards longer than anything made in the twenty years since.

That is the point about these records: they seem almost unassailable. Chamberlain, for example, broke his own record of 78 when he had his 100-point game; the best performance by another player is David Thompson's 73 points against the Detroit Pistons on April 9, 1978.

Perhaps the most striking example of this phenomenon at work would be Bob Beamon's amazing 29-foot-2½-inch long jump during the Mexico Olympics in 1968. In an event in which advances are made in quarter inches and very rarely, Beamon jumped more than a foot over the previous mark—"jumping into the next century," as a felicitous phrase in *Sports Illustrated* described it. For a number of years, no other long-jumper placed in the range of 28 to 29 feet; Beamon's entry looked like a printer's error in the record books.

What is odd is that Beamon—because he had achieved the unconscious state one looks for in *ki*, *ch'i*, *prana*, whichever—was not really aware of what he had done. I interviewed him some time later. I asked him if perhaps he had a mental catalyst, a spur to help him jump so far, if he imagined something snapping at his heels, a pack of wolves? He shook his head. No. Nothing like that. His mind was blank. He told me that he had hopped out of

the sawdust of the pit knowing that he had made a good
jump, but nothing about the jump struck him as extraordinary. He looked across the infield grass at the scoreboard, where the distances were measured in meters
rather than inches, and began to transpose the figures to
see how he had done. The roar of the crowd startled him.
He looked around to see what they were cheering—perhaps a pole vault somewhere in the arena—and realized
that the stands close to the track were emptying and that a
crowd was coming for *him*, arms outstretched, eyes shining with excitement. Abruptly, he was aloft on their
shoulders, being borne around the arena in triumph. It
was frightening, he told me, because the reason for all this
was not clearly set in his mind. He kept calling down from
the shoulders of his supporters to find out exactly what he
had done.

Bill Russell of the Boston Celtics once told me an extraordinary thing—that often players from the opposing
team get in the zone and "we'd *all* levitate," as he put it.
He would get so involved in the magic of what was going
on that he'd think, This is *it!* We've got to keep this going.
When the players made spectacular shots, whether a
Celtic or someone from the other team, he wanted the
shots to fall. It didn't make any difference who finally
won the game. The phenomenon happened rarely, but
when it did, Russell would get chills up and down his
spine. Once, the referee had blown a foul against the opposing team and he had *complained*. The referee's jaw
dropped. What Russell couldn't explain was that the foul
call had broken the spell and dropped everything back to
normalcy. It was a private feeling—something he never
tried to explain to his teammates, especially the part
about its not bothering him to lose if the teams were "levi-

tating." "I literally didn't care," he once said. "If we'd lost and we'd had minutes in that state I'd still be as free and high as a sky hawk." Indeed, it was the thought that during the game the players might possibly loft into this "sweet" time that was in large part his motivation to get back on the floor game after game.

Bill Bradley of the New York Knicks also spoke of this—the blending of human forces at the right time and in the right degree: "The experience is one of beautiful isolation . . . it goes beyond the ecstasy of victory."

■ ■ ■

BEING IN THE zone is a phenomenon one can experience in other professions—especially those in which bursts of creative energy occur. One would guess that "absent-minded" scientists and theorists spend a lot of time in it. Archimedes was stepping not only into a bath but into the zone when he figured out that an object submerged in water displaces its own volume, and was so pleased with himself that he ran into the street naked, shouting "Eureka! Eureka!" He was almost surely in the zone when he was run through by a Roman soldier after the Battle of Syracuse, oblivious to everything that was happening around him while working on a mathematical figure in the sand.

The literary world is full of examples of creative-energy surges that seem to have little or no connection with the conscious mind. One reads that Robert Louis Stevenson's plots were provided for him in his dreams by what he called his "Brownies." Hervey Allen, the author of the big, steamy best-seller *Anthony Adverse*, spoke of an angel-like creature that danced along his pen when he wrote—a kind of metaphysical recorder. Jean Cocteau said in an interview, "I feel myself inhabited by a force or being—very little known to me. It gives the orders; I follow."

Ernest Hemingway, in an interview I did with him, described a day in Madrid when the bullfights were snowed out and he found himself—though this wasn't the way he put it—in the zone. "First I wrote 'The Killers,' which I'd tried to write before and failed. Then after lunch I got in bed to keep warm and wrote 'Today Is Friday.' I had so much juice I thought maybe I was going crazy, and I had about six other stories to write. So I got dressed and walked to Fornos, the old bullfighters' cafe, and drank coffee, and then came back and wrote 'Ten Indians.' This made me very sad, and I drank some brandy and went to sleep. I'd forgotten to eat, and one of the waiters brought me up some bacalao and a small steak and fried potatoes and a bottle of Valdepeñas.

"The woman who ran the pension was always worried that I did not eat enough, and she had sent the waiter. I remember sitting up in bed and eating, drinking the Valdepeñas. The waiter said he would bring up another bottle. He said the señora wanted to know if I was going to write all night. I said no, I thought I would lay off for a while. 'Why don't you try to write one more?' the waiter asked. 'I'm only supposed to write one,' I said. 'Nonsense,' he said. 'You could write six.' 'I'll try tomorrow,' I said. 'Try it tonight,' he said. 'What do you think the old woman sent the food up for?'

" 'I'm tired,' I told him. 'Nonsense,' he said (the word was not *nonsense*). 'You tired after three miserable little stories? Translate me one.'

" 'Leave me alone,' I said. 'How am I going to write if you don't leave me alone?' So I sat up in bed and drank the Valdepeñas and thought what a hell of a writer I was if the first story was as good as I'd hoped."

7

To HELP ME sneak into the zone, a friend of mine has sent a catalog of inspirational tapes. The face of Dr. Paul Tuthill is on the cover—young, with a Freud-like beard and a pleasant, confident smile. In the catalog he quotes Thoreau: "Each of us has a Genius within us, waiting to be released."

Aha!

This is done, the catalog would have me believe, through subliminal messages—the subconscious hears the messages, which are synchronized and hidden within the music. The sports available did not include horseshoes, though boxing, skiing, bowling, weight lifting, and racquetball were listed. So I picked bowling since the arm motion is similar. I also ordered "Self-Confidence" and "Defeating Discouragement." The musical selections included bluegrass, country, reggae, classical. I picked "Inspirational Flute," which the catalog informed me combines flute sounds with "the natural rhythms of a babbling brook" to lift one above "the humdrum thoughts of everyday."

The catalog reports what the subliminal messages are if the sounds of the flute with its babbling brook rhythms were scraped away. Letters of certification attest that these messages are indeed there. They struck me, frankly, as somewhat peremptory and unimaginative. The stop-smoking tape apparently intones incessantly "Smoking stinks!" The tape entitled "Stop Math Anxiety" has as one of its subliminal messages "Math is easy!"

The catalog makes the tapes, though, sound extremely potent. Indeed, there is a warning about using two of them ("Maximum Strength" and "Stop Smoking") at the same time. "Each is a difficult challenge and should be addressed individually."

The tapes I ordered have arrived, and I play them on occasion. My friend asked me if I thought they were helpful. I said I didn't know. "A lot of flute music," I said. "It's hard to tell whether I have been lifted above the humdrum thoughts of everyday."

"What's that?"

"Never mind," I said. "I guess we'll find out in the Rose Garden if they worked."

■　■　■

BOOKSELLERS TELL US that eight percent of their shelves are devoted to self-help books—that the stocks of such things far outnumber the books devoted to poetry, art, travel, sport, whatever. Having listened to some inspirational tapes, I thought I should browse through the self-help shelves to see if by chance there was anything on them of value. Since I had little hope of running across a pertinent title (*Horseshoes—A Self-Hypnotic Way to Success?*) I took home rather a random selection.

What I hoped to find were concrete exercises to strengthen my resolve . . . prescriptions for personal excellence. By far the most arresting of these was in a book entitled *Unlimited Power* by Anthony Robbins. An impressive figure himself (6 feet 6 inches, 250 pounds) he gives seminars—these announced by the slogan "Unleash the Powers Within You"—often concluded by having his listeners walk barefoot across a fifteen-foot bed of hot coals! "Advanced groups" are taken across *forty* feet. The firewalk is used as a kind of real-life metaphor—which the author calls an "exercise in belief." To cross it is to take effective action in spite of any fear one might have.

Robbins calls this a "fun way" to learn how to change one's physiology so that walking on fire is transformed from something terrifying to something one can do.

Wow! It occurred to me (as it would to anyone) to wonder what happens to those who teeter on the brink of the coal pit and suddenly decide it's not for them—"fun way" or not—especially with the looming figure of the outsized author coming up behind. The answer is given midway in a chapter called "Physiology: The Avenue of Excellence." The author asks, "What do I do with a shaking, crying, frozen person shrieking on the edge of the bed of coals? One thing I can do is change his internal representations. I can have him think of how he will feel after having walked successfully and healthfully to the other side of the coals. This causes him to create an internal representation that changes his physiology. In a matter of two to four seconds, the person is in a resourceful state— you can see him change his breathing and facial expression. I then tell him to go, and the same person who was paralyzed with fear a split second earlier now walks purposefully over the coals and celebrates on the other side. . . . My other choice—one that's more efficient when someone is totally panicked in front of the coals—is to change his physiology. . . . So I take this crying person and have him look up. By doing this, he begins to access the visual aspects of his neurology instead of his kinesthetic. Almost immediately, he stops crying. Try this for yourself; if you are upset or crying and want to stop, look up. Put your shoulders back and get into a visual state. Your feelings will change almost immediately."

Presumably this "totally panicked" person, with his shoulders back, head high, made it across the coals. There are no failures mentioned in *Unlimited Power*. To get his audiences to act as if they know they are going to succeed, Robbins gets them "jumping up and down . . . roaring like lions . . . puffing up their chests . . . strutting like peacocks."

Hoping to find something less frenetic, in a chapter late in the book called "Anchoring Yourself to Success" I came across a paragraph that seemed more my speed: "Stand the way you did when you were totally confident," I was asked. "At the peak of that feeling, make a fist and say 'Yes!' with a strength and certainty. Breathe the way you did when you were totally confident. Again make the same fist and say 'Yes!' in the same tonality. Now speak in the tone of a person with total confidence and control. As you do this, create the same fist and then say, 'Yes!' in the same way."

This simple act apparently mobilizes one's most productive energies. If one has trouble remembering one's last state of total confidence (a problem quite pertinent in my case) one is urged to *imagine* such a moment. "Then, at the height of that experience," Robbins writes, "gently make a fist and say, 'Yes!' in a powerful tone of voice.

"I want you to actually do this," Robbins insists. "Just reading about it won't help. Doing it will work wonders."

So I tried it. A fist. "Yes!" The cat looked up from the windowsill.

■ ■ ■

TALKING TO ONESELF is an exercise utilized in most of the books I had selected. *What to Say When You Talk to Yourself,* a work by Shad Helmstetter, starts things off with the arresting statement that as much as 77 percent of what you tell yourself may be working *against* you. The thrust of his book is that you must reverse "negative programming" and "fill your life with new vital energy."

His notion, in brief, is that the brain is like a complex computer into which are fed negative impulses as a child—don't do this, don't do that—until finally the brain accepts these commands and acts accordingly. This results in negative self-talk—such as "I can't remember names," "I'm just no good at math," "I just can't take it any more," "Everything I touch turns to bleep."

Well and good. Helmstetter's solution is that negative programming can be erased with conscious positives. He gives an extraordinary example of how to go about this. A smoker trying to quit is urged to say aloud in the course of lighting up a cigarette: "I never smoke!" This is to be stated even in the company of other people, standing around, say, at a cocktail party. Helmstetter does admit that if you follow what he suggests, "your friends are going to think you're a little strange." I'll say! As for myself, I simply don't have the courage to do what he recommends—to dig into a chocolate mousse at a fancy dinner party and announce loudly to the table: "I never eat chocolate mousse!" It may be that my brain does indeed slowly begin to digest this, and that eventually I won't eat chocolate or sweets. But in the meantime I would guess the dinner invitations would be few and far between.

Certainly, it was hard for me to imagine transposing the Helmstetter theory to the Bush horseshoe match . . . to proclaim loudly after a bad shot, "I don't miss!" Or "I throw perfect ringers." The Secret Service would begin to close in after much more of this.

A book called *Born to Win* (the "landmark bestseller" by Muriel James and Dorothy Jongeward, both Ph.D.s) espouses a wildly opposite approach—that the way to deal with feelings of inadequacy is to express them. Here's a typical example:

> Talk to yourself about how inadequate and stupid you are.
> Look stupid. Exaggerate your facial expression.
> Acting stupid and inept, move around the room.
> NOW REVERSE YOUR FEELINGS
> Look yourself squarely in the face in the mirror and say, "I'm O.K."
> Say this aloud every day for at least a week and silently to yourself whenever you catch your reflection in a glass or mirror. Continue this until the "I'm O.K." feels good.

There was a lot of this—expressing inadequacy and then "reversing feelings." For example, under the heading *fear* it was suggested that I make a list of things and people I feared. I did so, putting another loss to the president at horseshoes at the top of the list. Then came the "reversing of feelings"—to become the opposite of frightened, *fierce*. I was urged to "look fierce enough to make someone [Bush?] scared of you," to "move around the room being fierce toward objects [horseshoes?] in the room. Feel your power when being fierce." I tried a bit of this. There weren't any horseshoes in the room, so I substituted a hairbrush—being terrified of it at first ("oh no, don't! don't!") and then (reversing my feelings) picking it up and hurling the hairbrush into the fireplace.

"Now how do you feel?" the book asks.

About the same, frankly. A little foolish.

■ ■ ■

I HAVE TURNED from the somewhat homeopathic measures of the self-help books to an old friend, Peter Buterakos, a cemetery-plot salesman from Flint, Michigan. Somewhat resembling a barrel-chested elf, he is famous throughout the Midwest for his inspirational speeches and especially his wild bursts of cajolery. I heard him give a speech on business administration before 4,500 in Flint that went on for more than an hour. He punctuated what he was saying by tossing various props out from the stage, including live pigs ("there are pigs in the business world!"); rubber daggers, blood-red at the tips ("at the top, people are waiting to stab you in the back!"); and rubber snakes ("competition can turn good men into snakes!"). He finished off his talk by plunging through a mock brick wall wearing a Superman outfit to demonstrate that "anything can be overcome."

Despite his small stature, he calls himself, and just about everyone else as well, "Big Man."

The phone rings.

"Big Man?"

His voice is so high and imperious that the receiver must be moved back from the ear.

"Er—yes?"

"Big Man! It's the Big Man, etc., etc. . . ."

I had met him not long after I had been with the Detroit Lions. He had come to training camp to give an inspirational talk, during which he had set off a cherry bomb ("life is full of abrupt changes"). It had rolled behind him and blown a big chunk of plaster out of the wall. Joe Schmidt, then the Lions coach, liked to say that Buterakos kept his audiences not only on the edge of their seats but usually two or three feet above them.

I telephoned him.

"Big Man," I said. "I'm going down to play horseshoes with the president."

The news didn't surprise him at all. "Why not, Big Man!" he shouted.

"I need a boost, Big Man," I said. "I need some ideas."

"You need to throw him off balance, Big Man," Buterakos said. "Blow his mind. Get him kind of uneasy, so he's even nervous picking up a horseshoe. Right?"

"Yes, Big Man," I said. "But remember that the Secret Service is standing around."

"Well, Big Man," Buterakos said, "I'd start off by calling him Lefty."

"Lefty?"

"He's left-handed, isn't he? If he isn't, Big Man, it's even better. Blow his mind. Then what you do when you're warming up is to pick up a horseshoe and lob it through a window of the White House. Then you turn and apologize. You say, 'Lefty, I hardly know my own strength today. I'm all pumped up. I've got the strength of Samson.' "

"Well . . . "

"Hey, get this, Big Man! When you arrive at the White House you're wearing all the uniforms from the teams you've played with. Wear your Detroit Lions football helmet. You shake hands with the president. Then you take off the helmet and under that you're wearing a New York Yankees cap. You raced cars, didn't you?"

"Well . . . "

"You're wearing an asbestos suit, bright red. You climb out of that and you're wearing your Boston Celtics T-shirt with your name on the back. You should wear a pair of skates out to the horseshoes."

"A pair . . . "

"You played for the Bruins, right? It'll blow Bush's mind. He'll ask, 'What are you wearing those things for?' You tell him, 'Lefty, I just got these skates *sharpened*. I can stop on a *dime*.' "

I tried to interrupt. "Hey, Big Man . . . "

"Listen to this, Big Man! You bring two people to the White House with you. Guess who."

"Who?"

"Mike Tyson." He paused for emphasis. "And the Hulk."

"They may have to carry me in," I ventured. "What with those skates and all. I have very weak ankles."

"Why not?" he shouted. "They lift you up under the elbows—Tyson and the Hulk—and they carry you out to the horseshoes like you're a kind of valuable weapon!

"Then what you do is bring a high school band with you, not a good one, Big Man, but one that's only been practicing for about a week. They know maybe two or three tunes—'Pop Goes the Weasel' and 'The Star-Spangled Banner.' Blow his mind! The music sheets always fall off those little stands, right? And get *this*, Big Man!"

"What?"

"You bring your own horseshoes," he shouted over the phone. "You say, 'Lefty, I don't trust your White House shoes. I've brought my own!' Tyson and the Hulk start pulling on a rope and from around a bush comes the biggest goddamn horse you ever saw in your life—a Percheron type of animal. It comes clomping in wearing the shoes you'll be using. It'll blow the president's mind!"

"How do I get them off?" I asked innocently.

"Hell, Big Man, you get the Hulk to topple that horse right over and he and Tyson *wrench* the shoes off the horse's feet and hand 'em to you. You tell the president, 'Nossir, nobody, I mean *nobody*, is goin' to tamper with my shoes.'"

I told him I was wanted on the other phone. "Thank you, Big Man," I said. "I'll be turning all this over in my mind."

He was still chattering away when I hung up.

8

IT OCCURRED TO me that Red Auerbach, the great Celtic basketball coach, would be interesting to talk to about the X Factor—an appropriate companion piece to what Bill Curry had told me about Vince Lombardi. He had left coaching the Celtics for the general manager's job when I joined the team briefly in 1969 in a participatory-journalism stint. That was the year we—if I may put it that way—won the NBA championship. I sat next to Auerbach in the stands for the seventh game of the series in Los Angeles. A great cluster of balloons hung above the court, high in the rafters of the Forum; the Lakers with Wilt Chamberlain, Elgin Baylor, Jerry West and company were heavily favored to win. The game was close. The clinching basket was a shot of Don Nelson's that hit the back rim, bounced several feet straight up, and then dropped down through the net. Auerbach lit his victory cigar—a famous signature gesture of his—just at the final buzzer. He took a puff or two, upon which a young Laker woman fan, her face contorted with fury—I got a good, startled look at her—raised an aerosol can of shaving cream and doused the cigar with a thick glob of white foam. It was about the only time I ever saw Auerbach slightly flustered.

I went down to Washington, D.C., to see him in his apartment there. The place is a repository of Celtic history—the walls covered with framed photographs and cartoons of his regime's stars: Bill Russell, John Havlicek, Tom Heinsohn, Sam Jones among them; those of Auerbach invariably show him with his cigar. When I mentioned what had happened in Los Angeles, he shook his head and smiled ruefully.

"Crazy city."

"Tell me about the cigars."

"I used to smoke cigars on the bench. I lit up a cigar one time and they took pictures. Finally the commissioner called up and said that I couldn't smoke cigars on the bench. I said, 'What's this, an airplane?' And that shut him up. So it became a victory-type thing—lighting up a cigar when a win was obvious."

He doesn't do it any more in the Garden—smoking is prohibited there. He lights up in a restaurant with the far-fetched name Legal Seafoods where the menu reads "no cigar smoking in the dining room except for Red Auerbach."

He offered me a cigar which I politely declined. I went on to describe the X Factor and asked how it contributed to the opportunity to light up so many of those victory cigars.

"Yeah . . . we must have had a lot of it . . . eight championships in a row. But each year I had to motivate them. In the fall I made sure they came ready to play. I'd call them together and I'd say, 'Good summer? Feel good to be a member of the best basketball team in the world? Go around with your chest puffed up? Great, great feeling, isn't it? But now that's in the past, like yesterday's newspaper. Now they're out to get you. You're the world champions and they're going to be motivated sky-high to beat you. The only way to keep them from doing that is to meet them head-on. If you're going to count your championships, and your money in the bank, and say to yourself that the ball's got my name on it, and therefore anytime there's a loose ball it's going to pop into my hands, why you're going to get *killed*. The ball doesn't have your name on it; it has the commissioner's name on it. You want that ball, you've got to go and get it!' "

"What about Celtic pride," I asked. "How much is that a factor?"

"I always firmly believed in establishing an alumni situation," he said. "I wanted players, if they played for the Celtics, always to remember it—whether winning or not that they'd be treated as people . . . not as a number who the tail end of a career would be got rid of or traded. We had more people start and finish their careers with us than the whole league combined. Players who played for other teams come to us in the twilight of their careers and most of them, like Paul Silas, for example, only talk about the time they were with Boston. They are Boston Celtic people. We throw a retirement day for them, hang the flag in the rafters."

"What happens when a player doesn't fit into this sort of atmosphere?"

"You've got to get rid of them," Red said. "They are invariably players who put individual accomplishment before a team concept."

"Does this mean you wouldn't rely on statistics?"

Red snorted. "The only true statistic in basketball is free throws," he said. "Everything else is ridiculous. Even the stat of steals is misleading. It doesn't list the steal you try for, miss, and the guy scores. Statistics don't record the shots made during the garbage time at the end of a blowout. Or shots made in the clutch. Or whether a player has the guts to take a key shot. Or how a player does defensively. Does he box out, or not box out? You can't measure such things."

"Is it possible to change someone who at first doesn't seem to fit into the Celtic mode?" I asked.

Red began talking about Bill Walton, the great center from the Trail Blazers who had come to Boston in the twilight of his career. "I had to lay it out beforehand to him that Larry Bird was the kingpin and that he would not even be the seventh player coming off the bench. So I said to him, 'Don't get the wrong idea about what we want you for. You don't have to score. You don't have to be the star. You're in there to get the ball—rebound, play the defense, run the court, and if you score, great, it's a big plus. But if you don't score, don't worry about it.' Bill was relieved. He thought if he didn't score double figures in every game he was going to be benched permanently and nobody would love him . . . all that kind of stuff. I did the same thing with Bill Russell. I told him, 'Bill, I've got plenty of firepower with Cousy, Heinsohn, Sharman . . . you go out, control the boards, get the ball to them, and I don't care if you never score a point.' We were so much a team that it was a way of life. You know what K. C. Jones once said about Willie Naulls? That when he came from the New York Knickerbockers he didn't know there were four other men until he joined the Celtics.''

I asked what the main lessons were that one learned as a coach over the years.

Red was emphatic. "It's important not to put yourself, certainly in *your* mind, up on a big pedestal. Every once in a while I'd blame myself for the loss of a game. 'I wasn't up for it,' I'd tell them. 'My work on the bench was shitty. I really stunk.' It worked. For example, after a game I'd sit on a stool in the locker room and meet the press for about five minutes. Then I'd say, 'See you later. Talk to the players.' For me it was always our ballclub, not my ballclub. You can't be too careful. There was a coach, Al Cervi, a great player, who had the Syracuse team—a real tough guy—and when the season was over, the players voted on the distribution of the playoff money. They voted him out! Ten to one. Cervi got mad and began yelling about it, so Dolph Schayes got up and said, 'I'm changing my vote. Now it's eleven to one.' The problem with Cervi was that he was one of those guys who when his team won, it was 'I' won. When they lost it was 'you' lost.

"Another thing I learned is the mistake most coaches make. They overcoach. Also, they like to hear the sound of their own voice, so they overtalk. They love meetings. There's no need to do that sort of thing with guys that have been around for five or six years. If I don't adjust, the players'll get tired of my voice, my philosophy, and they'll turn me off. I constantly had to think of how to maintain the motivation and keep their respect and attention. There were many ways to do this. I lessened the practices. I lessened my conversation. I had them teach the new guys.''

I said that I was always surprised to see a coach at the end of a game designing a play on a clipboard, his players grouped around.

Red laughed and said that half of them weren't paying attention anyway. "I never brought out a clipboard and all that bullshit," he went on. "What the hell have they been doing all year? If I were a player I'd get nervous— being given a new play with ten seconds to go. I tried to have my players smart. I'd group them around and say, 'There are twelve seconds to go. We do the 2-play. It takes eight seconds. Get it in, run the 2-play. Get a shot. Execute!' "

I asked how many plays the Celtics had.

"Six," Red said. "Of course each one of these has variations, backdoors, reverses, and so on—a total of about twenty—but all run off six basic patterns. Very simple."

I wondered how much input the players themselves were able to offer. Do they add to the X Factor?

Red nodded. He said, "I always told my players, if you've got something out there, let us know. I don't want this guy taking over the huddle, but he'll say, real softly, 'This guy is overplaying me. I think I can backdoor him.' So I say, 'Let's try it.' Because I have always been of the opinion that my players are college graduates, in their late twenties and thirties, so why treat them like kids with no brains. So whenever they wanted me to try something, I'd try it." He paused. "Except one time," he said with a smile. "Bill Sharmon came over to me one day and he said that the other team knew our plays. 'Everybody knows our numbers.' I told him it didn't make any difference. I said, 'How can they stop it? They don't know whether you're going to reverse it or not. So what?' But he said that he'd feel better if we could change the numbers.

So I said, 'All right, we'll try it. We have six plays. We'll jump the numbers up so that the 1-play becomes the 2-play and so on.' I knew it wouldn't work. But I gave them half a practice in which we used the new numbering system. So we have a game the next day. One guy says, 'Let's do a 3.' So two guys do the 3 and the other three forget, and it's all fucked up. So I don't say anything. They do it again. And they screw up. And again. Finally I called a time-out. They came to the bench and I told them to put their heads down real close like I was going to whisper something to them. I took my hand, like this, and I slapped them across their faces. 'Now, erase all that from your mind. From now on a 1 is a 1, and a 2 is a 2.' They all laughed like hell."

"Do you have to be liked?"

Red snorted again. "No way. A team must respect the coach as a person and a knowledgeable guy. But no coach in basketball can keep all his players happy. You have a squad of twelve, fourteen players, and you only start five. So there are at least seven players who don't like you because you have in essence discriminated against their ability. If you have, as some college coaches happen to, three seven-footers, two of those guys are asking themselves, 'Why did I come here? I could have been a star someplace else.'

"So no coach can be totally liked by his players. I always wanted players to owe me. Very important this. In twenty years of coaching I never fined any of my guys. Well, one time I fined Sam Jones five dollars. He had broken one of my dumb rules which was, 'Don't let me catch you eating pancakes on the day of a game.' We had come in late at night into Syracuse or Rochester, some place like that, and after I had registered the players in the hotel, everyone went out to eat since it was late, one in the morning, and I walked into the restaurant and there was Sam Jones eating pancakes. I said, 'Sam, that'll cost you five dollars.' He looked up and said, 'Well, I might as well finish them.' He picked up his fork. I said, 'Sam, that's five dollars a *bite*.' So he threw his fork down and stormed out. I never collected the five dollars. What's the point? Did he do it on purpose to spite me? No, it was late and he was hungry. But still, he broke the rules and now he owes me one. I remember once we had a great blizzard in Boston, which all the players pushed their way through to get to the Boston Garden. All except Bill Russell, then the player-coach. We had no assistant coaches. So I came out of the stands to run the team from the bench. We were playing San Francisco. Fifteen seconds to go, fifteen points ahead and in walks Russell with his scarf, his big hat, and he smiles and says, 'We're winning.' I said, 'Where the hell were you?' 'Blizzard,' he said. 'Couldn't get in.' 'God damn it,' I said. 'John Havlicek walked four miles to get here. You and your damn Lamborghini with its six carburetors couldn't make it?' I kept it up. 'Bill Russell,' I said, 'when you're not here, two people are not here—Bill Russell the coach, and Bill Russell the player.' I kept after him—not fining him, but to make sure that he felt he owed me one. I wanted him to owe me for the next game. And as a result the next day we killed them."

I asked how friendly a coach could ever be with his players.

Red said that he had a theory from way back that he would never go over to a player's house for dinner. "How can you go to a guy's house, play with his kids, have him fix you dinner, and then two days later you gotta fire him. Or trade him. So I would tell the players, 'I'm very appreciative, but don't invite me.' Fraternization is something you really have to worry about. One of the big problems are the wives. I remember a case involving a party the Baltimore Bullets had back in the '50s. One of the wives had a couple of drinks and went after this other player's wife: 'The reason your husband makes so many shots is that my husband feeds him the ball. But your husband never feeds it back.' This went on and on. Then it happened: the two wives got into a big fight in Seattle and the upshot was that those two players were traded."

Red leaned forward and switched on the television set. He wanted to watch the final set of a tennis match. When it was done, he gave me a short tour of the apartment—showing me his considerable collection of letter-openers, swords from Burma, objects beautifully wrought in ivory, mementos from his trips around the world. His wife is a collector as well—statuettes of boxer dogs, some in costumes and dresses, shelf on shelf of them.

I told him about my upcoming horseshoe match with the president—that I felt I was making the mistake of not preparing for it sufficiently.

Red shrugged. "I always got my guys in shape before the season started. We'd train hard and we'd always get a jump on the other guys, move out in front 15–1, 16–2, so they were always playing catch-up." He paused before a large standing globe of the world and revolved it slightly. "But you don't need to do that . . . to train to beat the president isn't worth it. It's a social thing. Of course, it's according to how important it is to you . . . "

I didn't go into it. I thanked him. I said I hoped he'd let

me know when the Celtics came to New York. Perhaps we could go to the Garden together.

He shook his head. No, he always got hassled there. "Crazy city," he said.

9

THE OTHER DAY I took out a sheaf of notes collected about the X Factor—a year's worth of material from reading or from conversations with various champions to get myself ready for the big horseshoe match. As I went through them, it occurred to me to rearrange them in the form of a Q and A interview with an imaginary expert on such matters. This is what I have done and it follows.

I see the person being interviewed hardly as myself, indeed not at all, but rather as an elderly and worldly gentleman of superb prowess and proportions, noble head and all, who has risen from humble circumstances (a farm boy in Iowa) and adversity (a spot of polio perhaps, the loss of a finger in a haying accident, an alcoholic father) to become a great athlete at Notre Dame, a Rhodes scholar at Oxford, this followed by a twin career as a centerfielder for the San Francisco Seals and a linebacker for the New York Giants, an Olympic decathalon champion . . . retiring unscarred and at his prime, immediately to become a star at J. P. Morgan, soon its president, along with being a trustee of just about every worthy academic and artistic institution, thought of as being a candidate for governor, etc. etc.

He is being interviewed in his library, a golden retriever snoring softly at his feet. The lighting is muted. The silver cups and bowls reflect the glow from the fire. His Heisman Trophy stands in a corner.

Frankly, he is not a particularly pleasant gentleman—arch and rather superior. The interviewer is somewhat intimidated, both by him and the surroundings. He is waved to a leather chair.

Q: You are very kind to see me.

A: I understand you are about to play a game of horseshoes with the president which you would like to win. Frankly, your best bet would be to allow me to go in your stead. Though I have never picked up a horseshoe—I have always considered horseshoes a plebian game and am surprised a Republican president dabbles in it—I have no doubt I would emerge from the horseshoe pit (what an ugly appellation!) victorious. I say this because I don't believe in false modesty. Confidence is essential in your situation. I am reminded that in his early years Winston Churchill was given the chance to preview an upcoming article about himself. The report had written "cheers" to describe an audience's reaction to a speech. Churchill had crossed this out and substituted "loud and prolonged applause."

May I offer another example of confidence, if not cockiness. The minor league Saginaw baseball team, a

Detroit farm club, had a brassy young pitcher in the old days who had a 20–2 record, something like that, and boasted he could handle Ty Cobb. In fact, he wrote the Tiger front office and said as much. They admired his spunk, so they invited him down to Briggs Stadium, sent him out to the pitcher's mound with a bag of baseballs, and persuaded Cobb to go to the plate for five pitches or so. Cobb hit five terrific shots off him. They asked the kid what he thought about that. He replied: "Hell, I don't believe that's Cobb!"

Compare Grego Piatigorsky, the great cellist, who used to pump himself up before a concert by telling himself, "Don't be nervous, Grischa. You are the great Piatigorsky."

Someone once asked him, "Does it help?"

"No," he said. "I don't believe myself."

Q: Why "compare"?

A: Because I suspect your thought process lacks confidence. You probably think you are going to lose in your horseshoe match. But then you must remember that you are an amateur. The *Oxford English Dictionary*—the *OED* if you will—has essentially two definitions for that word: (l) hobbyist, (2) incompetent.

Q: I don't find this very helpful.

A: Let's be very frank. It's best to be *born* a great athlete. No doubt about it. Saves a lot of time and trouble. Your chances against the president would be considerably improved if you had been born a great athlete like me. First time I ever picked up a baseball as a tot I threw it and knocked a pot of beans off the kitchen stove. First time I ran a measured mile over an Iowan cornfield as a high school kid I came within a second of the state record. But let's not talk about me. Take Emil

Zatopek, the Czech long-distance runner. In the Olympics in Helsinki in 1952 wearing a white house-painter's cap, he won the 5,000 meters, the 10,000 meters, and then the marathon despite never having run the distance before. Asked for his impression of the latter he replied, "The marathon is a very boring race." Apparently to get over the boredom he would drop back and chat with runners struggling at the back of the pack. Imagine that! . . . to have someone range up alongside to start a conversation—what Helsinki restaurants would be worth a try that night after the race, say, or what books had one read recently—someone who had *never run the race before* . . . a weird burble of words from a man in a white house-painter's cap!

The funny thing about Zatopek was that he *looked* as though he was having a terrible time. I remember Red Smith once wrote about him: "Witnesses who have long since forgotten other events still wake up screaming in the dark when Emil the Terrible goes writhing through their dreams, gasping, groaning, clawing at his abdomen in horrible extremities of pain."

Or take Babe ("Don't-call-me-Mildred") Didrikson, the sensation of the 1932 Los Angeles Games. Great friend of mine. She held American, Olympic, or world records in five different track and field events. One headline about her read "Babe Breaks Records Easier Than Dishes." She wasn't as large as one might expect from such a power athlete—5 feet 6½ inches and 126 pounds—yet she was an All-American basketball player. She went to the pitcher's mound in an exhibition and struck out Joe DiMaggio. She could throw a baseball over 300 feet. She could punt a football 75 yards. And, of course, she became a legendary golfing champion. The first time she ever tried hitting a golf ball—this according to Grantland Rice—it went 250 yards. She won over eighty golf tournaments. Not only was she overwhelming at sports, she was a fine ballroom and adagio dancer (I did a turn or two with her at Roseland) and she could play the harmonica well enough to make a living at it. Paul Gallico of the New York *Daily News* once asked her if there were anything she *didn't* play."Yeah," she replied. "Dolls."

An absolute natural. Take the Olympics in Los Angeles in '32. The javelin throw. She knew very little about the technique of throwing the thing. She threw it flat, like a catcher pegging a throw to second, rather than in an arc. On her first throw of the three allowed in the competition, the javelin never went higher than 10 feet, but nevertheless came within 10 feet of the world record. She tore a tendon doing this, but the injury wasn't a factor because her competitors in their successive tosses never got closer than 6 inches to her mark. Things have changed, of course—techniques, training methods. These days, the German javelin thrower Petra Meier-Felke holds the world's record at 262 feet 5 inches—almost 120 feet farther than Babe's throw in those '32 Games. But don't kid yourself. The only woman even vaguely in the Babe's class was Stella Walsh, born Stanislawa Walasiewicz. She was the 100-meter sprint champion in 1932. Years later, an innocent bystander, she was killed in some kind of a robbery attempt. An autopsy disclosed that although she'd lived her entire life as a woman she was in fact biologically a man. That was *her* X Factor. Still not enough to beat the Babe!

Q: You might be interested to know that I went to the Colorado Springs Olympic Training Center to be tested to see if I was especially good at something athletic which I didn't know.

A: How quaint! And what did you find out?

Q: Well, that I'm a good exhaler and can kick more powerfully backwards than forwards . . .

A: And did they specify any events?

Q: Spurring a horse, perhaps. Somebody suggested I'd be awfully good as a bull in a bullfight.

A: Perfect!

Q: Look, this is not going well. True, I am not a born athlete like you or the Czech guy or Babe Didriksen. But it's me, not you or the Babe, who's the one playing horseshoes with the president. Perhaps you could be more constructive.

A: Well, you might work on some of your motivational impulses. Some are inspired. Sonny Liston's was that all that stood between him and a hot date with Lena Horne was the guy in the opposite corner waiting for the bell. Muhammad Ali had a device in the ring something like that but a little less extravagant. It had to do with an incident when he was a kid in Louisville and had saved up to buy a secondhand bicycle, which was then promptly stolen. Just about broke his heart. He wandered around Louisville looking for it that whole summer—just simmering, and he used to say that every time he got in the ring, he looked across at the other fighter and said to himself, There's the guy who stole my bicycle.

Q: I'm afraid I find it difficult to work up that kind of animosity towards Mr. Bush.

A: And to think you're of the opposing political party!

Well, how about this. Perhaps you should work up a kind of relationship with a horseshoe. Do you know who Al Feuerbach is?

Q: No.

A: Well, you should. World-class shot-putter. Great friend of mine. He felt it was important to have a near-symbiotic relationship with the object used in his sport. It's not uncommon. Football coaches often suggest, even order, their more butter-fingered players to carry a football everywhere with them—not only on the side-lines, but to classes, to the movie theater. In Feuerbach's case it was an iron ball. He kept such things around the house. In his bed. When he went out, he carried one with him in a purse that had flowers on it. He was being nice to it. I have no doubt that subconsciously he felt the shot would behave better when it left the heave of his shoulder in a track meet if he'd been nice to it. Wouldn't you agree?

Q: You're suggesting I carry a horseshoe around with me?

A: Why not? You could talk to it, take it to dinner. Order it a salad. The more you commune with a horseshoe, the better off you're likely to be. Do you know John McPhee's fine book about Bill Bradley of the Knicker-bockers which he titled *A Sense of Where You Are*? McPhee describes how Bradley had a basketball with him at all times, bouncing it down the corridors of an ocean liner on a transatlantic crossing—developing a sense of enormous familiarity with it. The title comes from an afternoon session in the Princeton gym where Bradley was keeping himself in shape for the Olympics, working in particular on an over-the-shoulder shot. He popped in a couple of these and then turned and told McPhee the shot wasn't as difficult as one might suppose, and to illustrate, he tossed the ball over his shoulder and into the basket while he was looking McPhee in the eye. He did it twice. His explanation was that when you've played basketball for a while, you don't need to look at the basket when you're that close . . . you develop *a sense of where you are.*

Q: You're inferring that I should spend a lot of time practicing. I promised myself that I would not do that—it wouldn't be fair to the president.

A: How absurd! Sportsmanship! Not applicable. I am instantly reminded of one of my dissertations at Oxford—on the so-called Seven Weeks War in 1866 between the Prussians and Italy on one side, and the Austrians on the other. In a naval battle, one of the Italian ships, commanded by the Conte di Persane— big believer in sportsmanship—closed with the Austrian flagship, which if memory serves was the *Ferdinand Max,* and damaged her badly. The Count's officers urged him to ram the enemy and finish him off, but he refused on the grounds that it wasn't "sporting" to do such a thing. A gentleman did not ram another gentleman's battleship unless it was in working order. While the Count was explaining this to his flag officer, he was himself rammed and sunk.

So I would recommend strongly in your case that you forget sportsmanship, at least in the sense you have of it. May I remind you of the Greeks. Pindar, the splendid lyric poet of the fifth century, said that the essential quality for an athlete of his time was expressed by the word *aidos*, a kind of code to which the athlete should adhere—a sense of respect, reverence, modesty, honor . . . qualities which disinguish the athlete from the bully. And yet *aidos* had very little to do with sportsmanship. In the Ancient Games there were prizes for coming in second and third—amphoras of oil, things like that—but there was never a tradition of shaking hands after a competition; winners were never congratulated by those they had beaten. Losers were looked upon with disdain, their hometowns disgraced. Pindar wrote of them, "By back ways they slink away sore smitten by misfortune. No sweet smile greets their return." After all, you know what Homer says in the *Odyssey* . . . that there is no greater glory for a man as long as he lives than that which he wins by his own hands and feet. An athlete's credo, what?

Q: And why not an organist's?

A: Don't get flip with me, my good man. The line is from the time when Odysseus was shipwrecked and rescued by the Phaeacians. It's described in Book VIII of the *Odyssey*. Do you know the story?

Q: No. I wish you wouldn't raise your eyebrows in that way.

A: I will try to be less astonished at your educational shortcomings. The story is this: Odysseus, somewhat the worse for wear because of the shipwreck, is being entertained by Alcinous, the king of the Phaeacians, at a great gala. A blind minstrel sings of the deeds of heroes, Odysseus among them. Afterwards, Alcinous suggests they all have a kind of gymkhana—a sporting event involving various footraces, boxing, wrestling matches, weight-throwing, and so on. Odysseus wearily agrees to this, provided he doesn't have to perform. So, a crowd of literally thousands moves off to a great field to watch. One of the contestants is Alcinous's son, Laodamus. He marvels at how athletic Odysseus seems—muscular thighs, bull neck, and so forth—and suggests that given these attributes, surely Odysseus would like to compete. It is here that Laodamus says the line I mentioned before. Actually, I prefer T. E. Lawrence's translation to Robert Fitzgerald's: "There is no surer fame in a man's own lifetime than that which he wins with his feet and his hands."

Apparently Odysseus doesn't agree. He shakes his head.

At this point a man named Euryalas, who had won the wrestling competition, begins to taunt Odysseus, calling him a second-rate ship's captain—after all he'd wrecked his ship. He chides him: "You are not a champion!"

Well, this is too much for Odysseus. He accuses Euryalas of being rude and also mindless. Done with that, he goes over and picks up an early version of the discus—a stone far heavier than any seen that afternoon—and hurls it further than the farthest mark. And nor is he finished. He challenges his hosts to box, to wrestle, whatever . . . he is *nettled*, to put it mildly, to be called a ninny.

All this quiets the Phaeacians down. No one can think of anything to say. Finally, the king apologizes in a most self-deprecatory way . . . admitting that his people are not particularly good fighters or wrestlers, and in truth they are far more interested in (and here I'm quoting our friend Lawrence's translation) "eating and harp-playing and dancing and changing of clothes and hot baths and beds."

Q: That is an interesting story, but I fail to see . . .

A: My dear fellow, it suggests that it might be wise if you got someone to persuade the president to criticize your horseshoe playing . . . to call you a "ninny." Nothing spurs a competitor to higher levels of play than to be called a ninny. That is why coaches are terrified of their players mouthing off and making derogatory statements to the press that the opposing coach can post on the clubhouse bulletin board. Of course, in your case it may be that you *prefer* eating and hot baths, etc. etc. and harp-playing and that you have more Phaeacian in your genetic makeup than the Odysseus-factor.

Q: I doubt I can find a way of getting George Bush to call me a ninny.

A: It looks as though you are destined to be a loser. May I give you an example of my favorite loser . . . present company excepted, of course. At the Olympic Games in Greece, Gardner Williams, an American swimmer, was poised to leap into the Bay of Zea in the Aegean for a middle-distance race—this, of course, before the days of Olympic pools, chlorine, and marked lanes. The starting gun went off. Gardner Williams jumped in, yelled "Jesu Christo!" as he hit the water, and immediately clambered out, complaining that it was too cold.

Let me give you another. In 1918 a rookie named Harry Heitman walked in for his major league debut as a pitcher with the Brooklyn Dodgers, gave up in succession a single, a triple, and a single . . . was relieved by the manager, went into the clubhouse, showered, left the ballpark for a recruiting station, and enlisted in the United States Navy. To hell with it, he said.

Q: I do not find this helpful.

A: Please be quiet. I see no reason for interrupting. I am thinking, or *trying* to think, of a fighter . . . oh yes, named Kid McCoy. He was knocked out by Joe Gans. When the Kid recovered in the dressing room, someone solicitously asked him how he felt. He said, "I'm not a fighter. I'm a lover."

Q: Perhaps that's a winner's remark.

A: Nonsense. With a comment like that, you don't collect little trophies like that one over there [the Heisman].

Q: So many of your observations . . . your suggestions are downers. I think what I need is something more upbeat . . . a pep talk.

A: Why not? One of the best pep-talk stories I've ever heard was one Bear Bryant used to tell—that a motivation specialist named Doc Rhodes gave such a rousing halftime talk to a Kentucky Wildcat team that a big tackle got steamed up and began bounding about the locker room banging into the walls and knocking over benches, raring to get at the opposition, which happened to be the Tennessee Vols. The trouble was that he wasn't first string or even second, and he wasn't sent into the game until the final quarter with Tennessee on the 15-yard line. He ran halfway out and then came running back to the sidelines to ask: "Hey, Coach, can Doc Rhodes talk at me again?"

Q: I fail to see . . .

A: All right. Let's be practical. Do you choke?

Q: Well, I don't expect to . . .

A: Let me tell you about Miloslav Mecir, the Czech tennis star. He was playing Jimmy Connors some years ago. It was not only one of Mecir's first big tournaments, but also he was playing a man who was one of his idols—a "lege" (for legend) as we say on the circuit. Mecir won the first set, was leading in the second, and then suddenly he couldn't *throw the ball up to serve*. He had to serve underhand! Lost that set and then the final set 6–0. Paralyzed! It wasn't that a tendon in his arm had snapped or anything like that. Mental-motor paralysis! Perhaps the thought of beating his idol unhinged him. Whatever. So it happens to the best of them.

Q: Are you suggesting that I'll swing my arm back and be unable to bring it forward to throw the horseshoe?

A: I don't see why not. Just in case, I have a young psychologist friend named Alexis Castori who's been working with Ivan Lendl on the kind of mental-focus exercise that'll keep you from choking. It works this way—to take a small object like a dime or a hairbrush, or in your case a horseshoe, whatever, and describe it aloud for five minutes. The idea behind this is that after doing this day after day Lendl can focus his mind on the tennis court like a laser beam without being bothered by outside interferences. True, I have on occasion thought of Lendl, a good friend of mine, being caught at this—by someone opening the door and seeing Lendl sitting on the edge of a bed, a dime between thumb and forefinger, staring at it, and soliloquizing like Hamlet with poor Yorick's skull. There could be alarm and concern for the fellow's sanity.

In any event, mental focus has much to do with success, whether it's tennis or horseshoes. Another friend of mine, Michael Murphy, in a book of his entitled *The Psychic Side of Sports,* describes a karate teacher, or "sensei," who won an arm-wrestling contest using only his *little finger.* The explanation for this was that using one finger put the sensei at an advantage because he was able to focus the same amount of strength into a smaller area.

Q: You're making fun of me. I really find all of this quite useless and you insufferable.

A: Calm down. You've awakened my golden retriever, Ch. Rob Roy McClellan. Actually, it may be that anger is just the thing to carry with you into the Rose Garden. There's an interesting book by Rex Lardner called *Out of the Bunker and into the Trees* in which the "Rosetta stone" of his revolutionary theory is that you hit a bad shot *because you do not get angry enough*. He lists a number of things to get into the proper state of fuming anger to take out to the golf course. Among them, as I recall, are busy signals at the other end of the phone, crooked bread one has to pry out of a toaster, people who whistle one's favorite tunes a bit off-key, and so on. Just the thought of any one of these is bound to add considerable yardage to one's drive off the tee. He adds in a chapter entitled "How to Apply Body English" that additional power can be obtained by the violent jerking up of the head. A valuable volume.

Q: I think this is quite enough. Thank you for your . . . help. I'm grateful for all this, though I have no idea of how to put any of it to use.

A: Ah, but you must try. Thomas Carlyle once said of Alfred Lord Tennyson: "Alfred is always carrying a bit of chaos around with him, and turning it into a bit of cosmos." Indeed, that is surely the poet's function in life, isn't it? It's quite the same whatever one's profession. Perhaps you can take what you have heard here, chaotic as it may seem, and use it to your benefit down in Washington. Frankly, I doubt it. Ah well, we must remember that nothing is more democratic than losing.

10

I WROTE A LETTER to the president saying that with spring weather coming my thoughts were increasingly turning to horseshoes and the prospect of the rematch. I didn't tell him about Dr. Tuthill's inspirational tapes or Peter Buterakos's big horse, and I certainly didn't tell him about my imaginary interview with the insufferable Heisman Trophy winner. Nor did I say that I had not touched a horseshoe since we had last played at the Naval Observatory. I did mention the X Factor and that I hoped we would have a chance to chat about it, even if briefly. Ready to leave New York at a moment's notice, I added that I had purchased a cowboy hat.

Within days a letter arrived from the White House. The president wrote he was so looking forward to the match that he was "already suited up in his National Horseshoe Pitchers Association jacket." The question was where to play and when. "Here [the White House] we could do it almost any day—after work, or skip lunch and tee it up. At Camp David we have a classic setup as well. . . . How about a biathlon: shoes and tennis doubles?"

We decided on Camp David. He asked me to bring anyone I wanted. I took my son, Taylor, who is thirteen. He was nervous about it. He found it hard to accept that he was facing a weekend with the president. "I don't know about this," he said.

"You can cheer me on at the horseshoes," I told him. Taylor's voice is breaking, often cracking in midword, so that with an exhortation such as "Come on, Dad!" the first word is a boy's soprano, clear as a bell, and the *Dad* deep, a kind of bassoon note. Perhaps this might throw the president off. Taylor is a good athlete, especially at tennis; he is the junior champion where he plays in the summer. "I'm sure you'll be involved," I said.

We left on a Saturday morning shuttle for Washington. I forgot my cowboy hat. Tall-crowned with a blossom of feathers in the front, it made me feel less a cowboy than a Las Vegas crapshooter.

"Damn!"

My son looked over.

"I forgot my hat."

He looked startled, which was not surprising since he has never known me to wear a hat.

"It was a cowboy model," I explained. "A good-luck hat. I've never worn it except to try it on, but I feel lost without it. My X Factor hat!"

It was raining heavily when we landed. Taylor and I were picked up at National Airport by a White House car for the drive to Camp David. There are no directional signs to the facility, which is in fact a military installation in the higher reaches of Maryland's Catoctin State Park.

The car wound up through the thick woods and stopped outside a high steel-mesh fence. A military guard stepped out of a guardhouse and inspected the underside of the car with a mirror on the end of a pole. Our driver was waved through. Beside me, Taylor was becoming increasingly nervous. It was his spring break and I suspect he would have preferred to be walking along a Florida beach with his friends and then turning to run for the sea for the first surf ride of his vacation.

The guest houses at Camp David are spread throughout the woods, painted pale green, each with a golf cart out in front, and also bicycles, bright baby blue. The guest houses are named after trees—Red Oak, Aspen. The communal house is called Laurel, which is where the guests meet for lunch and dinner and the president has his office. It is just a short distance down the macadam path. The paths were once riding trails, but Richard Nixon had them paved over, much to the disappointment of Ronald Reagan who liked to relax at Camp David astride a horse.

No sooner had we put our bags down than a quick knock sounded. We looked up expecting a functionary to help or advise in some way. The president was standing in the doorway wearing a tall cowboy hat. I stared at it. He ducked his head as he came in. I introduced him to Taylor. "You're going to have a great time," the president assured him in a loud, cheerful voice. "Lunch in half an hour. No ties. No coats. After lunch we start the sports."

He addressed all this to Taylor, as if the afternoon was a kind of conspiracy between them. "Yes, sir," Taylor said, looking up, his eyes shining with excitement.

Before lunch the president gave us a tour of his working quarters in Laurel. There was not much to see: a conference room, with its long mahogany table decorated with models of the presidential planes and helicopters down its length, and a pint-sized office barely able to contain more than four people at a time. There the president showed us a large framed map of the U.S.S.R. he had received from Gorbachev, which showed a kind of nooselike arrangement of symbols representing U.S. military bases encircling the Soviet Union—less a gift, perhaps, than a reminder of how threatened the Soviets felt. I asked how accurate the map was. "Very," the president replied.

In the center of the room, leaving even less space to get around in, was a glass case, which served as a coffee table. It enclosed a display of a small covey of quail crouched amid the autumn leaves around a stump, beautifully mounted and reflecting, of course, the president's love of quail-shooting. The president told us that Mrs. Bush—because of her love for animalkind—did not think much of the quail group, and that was why it had been relegated to the president's office.

"Here, Taylor. Let me show you something else Mrs. Bush doesn't approve of," the president said. In a small hallway just off his office he showed us a large framed cardboard cutout of a man's head and torso—the silhouette target used on pistol and rifle ranges. In the center of the torso were scrawled the names of Bush and Marc Cisneros—the latter a top American general in Panama. Cisneros had discovered it in Noriega's headquarters during the Panama operation and thought the president would like it. The cutout was bullet-ridden—20-odd holes, mostly in the head, fired from a 9-mm pistol about 15 feet or so away, presumably by Noriega. Cisneros had handwritten a description of the circumstances along one side of the cutout, ending with the salutation "Merry Christmas!"

"Wow!" Taylor said.

Also on the wall was a wicked-looking military knife removed from one of Noriega's "dignity" battalions, and next to it the original mug shot of Noriega snapped in the Miami jail. A true trophy wall!

"Wow," Taylor said again as we walked into the living room.

By chance, I caught sight of Dan Quayle's face on a television set murmuring in the corner of the living room.

"Look, sir," I said to the president. "It's your vice-president."

"Yes," the president said without turning his head. "He's back from South America."

He didn't seem at all interested. It struck me how divorced he seemed from all the complexities of his office. The desk in his office was bare except for a coffee-cup warmer. On the rare occasions when there was a phone message, it was a family matter. Increasingly, I had the feeling that Taylor and I were enjoying a weekend stay with a country squire who didn't have anything on his mind except perhaps how his prize springer spaniels were going to do in the local dog show. His weekends were completely for relaxation.

Lunch was announced. The entire house party had gathered—the president and his wife; his brother Jonathan, his wife, Jody, and their two sons, John Jr., who is at Wesleyan University, and Billy, who is a star lacrosse player and captain of his team at St. George's School; his daughter-in-law Margaret and her two children, Marshall, age four, and Walker, age four months. The only outsider besides Taylor and me was a young woman named Lloyd Hatcher, a friend of Margaret Bush and a recent graduate of the University of North Carolina, who was working on the White House staff. Young Walker Bush was passed around the room, as one might pass a salver of mints, to be inspected by family members. Dogs were underfoot—Millie, an English springer spaniel named after a Texas friend, Mildred Kerr. Millie succeeds a cocker spaniel named C. Fred, who was described by Mrs. Bush as being deaf toward the end of a long life and who would snap at anything not coming from the front. Millie's son Ranger was also on the premises. Both were constantly on the move, their claws skittering on the bare floors between the rugs. Millie carried a tennis ball between her teeth so that it seemed a natural extension of her face. The president took it from her and lobbed it across the room.

"Uh-oh."

He had hit Mrs. Bush, who was on the telephone with someone, on the side of the head.

Mrs. Bush hardly took notice. "George," she said into the phone, "just hit me on the side of the head with a tennis ball."

"Serious business," the president said.

We went in to lunch and started talking about buzz-words. I mentioned "Vic Damone," for victory. Barbara Bush laughed. She said that when the information about Vic Damone became public and got into the papers, they had met the Damones. Vic had thanked President Bush for the publicity; he was "getting started on a second career."

During lunch the president continued to make Taylor feel at home. Among other things, they talked about preparatory schools. The president mentioned that his attachment to Andover was far stronger than to Yale.

"Why is that, sir?" I asked.

The president shook his head ruefully. "Well, Yale burned me in effigy some years back. That tends to linger on."

The afternoon sports program (it was still raining heavily) started with bowling—a caravan of golf carts, black umbrellas raised, riding along the paths to a low-slung building, again pale green and hard to spot amid the trees. The president skipped the bowling (for a nap, we were told), but he joined us in midafternoon for the game called 'wallyball," which is volleyball played on a racquetball court. The president, who was wearing gray sweatpants and a T-shirt that read UNIVERSITY OF WASHINGTON SERVICE, lined up on the opposite side of the net with Taylor, Lloyd Hatcher, and a presidential aide named Tim, who was possessed of a hard off-sidewall serve that caused great confusion in the ranks of the opposition— myself, Jonathan Bush, and his two sons.

The noise within the confines of the court was deafening. As soon as the ball was in the air the uproar began— yells of encouragement, yelps of appreciation at good retrieves, each point ending with shouts of delight on one side of the net and moans of despair, apologies, and recrimination on the other. Our team—none of us had played wallyball before—was getting the worst of it. Across the net Taylor was playing with great spirit. His favorite athlete is Boris Becker; like him he tends to sprawl headlong after shots, skidding on the floor. The president beamed down at him. "Hey, Taylor!" he called out. Their team won six games. After each game the president called out, "How 'bout another?"

We played for more than two hours. Billy, one of Jonathan Bush's boys, went out with a sprained shoulder. That didn't stop the fray. A mammoth marine, or perhaps a Secret Service man, was hurried into action on our team. Eager to please, he sprang around the court. We won a game. "How 'bout another?" the president asked.

Finally he said, "Well, maybe that's enough." Handshakes, and then the president led us to the exercise room just off the racquetball court—Nautilus equipment, stationary bicycles, treadmills, rowing machines. Some of them were being used by military personnel—husky men with crew cuts who wore slightly embarrassed looks when the president walked in, as if they couldn't decide whether to spring off the machines to attention or to continue pumping away. The president nodded and spoke to some of them. He programmed a bicycle machine for Taylor. He tried one himself. When I left to get ready for dinner he was lying on his back, encompassed by an apparatus that was supposed to strengthen his lateral arm movement. He's thinking about the horseshoe match, it occurred to me.

Sunday morning the president and I got a chance to talk about the X Factor. I sat opposite him in his little office. When I mentioned the X Factor, the president immediately said that he knew what I was talking about. In his case he felt the X Factor had something to do with his reaction to crowds.

"Crowds, sir?"

He went on to say that thirty or forty years ago crowds had often affected him adversely. He described playing in what he called "one of those deadly pro-ams" on a golf course near New Orleans.

"I was partnered with Mike Souchak. In those days I was playing to an 11 handicap, which is pretty good. The crowds were getting bigger as we got near the 18th. I then shanked three shots in a row. Watching was a taxicab driver who must have left his cab on the street to come out to the golf course; he was still wearing his badge number—3280 or whatever—up on his cap. He'd seen me shank the first one, giggling behind his hand. After I shanked the second, and was stepping up to hit the third shot, which was about a half nine-iron, I heard him say (I've got rabbit ears) to the guy next to him, 'You really want to see somethin', watch *this* cat.' And I shanked it again! A lot of guffawing!

"Well, that was the situation then. In those days I found I did better one on one, *mano a mano*. With people watching, the pressure made me knuckle under. When I was about twelve or thirteen, playing in a country-club tournament, I ordered my aunt out of her seat at courtside because she was making too much noise."

"I can't imagine that you got away with it," I said.

"Of course not," the president said. "I had to write a long letter of apology. But that was all a long time ago. Since I got into politics and thus more comfortable with the roar of the crowd, it's been a 180-degree turn."

"You look forward to the pressures?"

"That's right. Rising to the occasion. Maturity has a lot to do with it, of course. When the horseshoe pit was inaugurated at the White House, with quite a crowd there, I was asked to throw a couple of shoes. It went through my mind, *well, suppose I step up and don't even get it in the clay.* I went ahead, and darned if I didn't get a couple of ringers." He grinned. "I quit immediately. Timing is very important."

"So the X Factor has a lot to do with what you gain from experience?"

"Learning how to fight back. They say you're 17 points down in the polls. So I'm going to show 'em. Fight back. I find that as the pressure mounts, the adrenaline flows, and it pushes you to be better. There's a relationship. Of course, you can have the adrenaline flowing and screw it up.

"It all goes back to what your mother taught you: do your best, try your hardest. It's funny, but here I am, the president of the United States, and that advice from my mother, who is highly competitive and loves sports, still affects almost everything I do—try your hardest, and if you know you're doing that, criticism rolls off like water off a duck's back. That would not have happened, incidentally, before the X Factor started working *for* me instead of against me. I got over it when I matured, got into the big leagues of politics."

I wondered how it was possible to face that barrage of comment every morning, the columns, the cartoons . . .

"You can't afford to bristle and get tense about it," the president said. "The parallel in sport is some guy yelling at you from the stands, or the coach in the locker room. You can't take it personally. You just determine, well, we'll show 'em."

"Do you think of politics as a kind of game?" I asked. "It has so many of the same metaphors."

"Campaigns, yes. But not so much in the day-to-day politics. If you're in a fight to sustain a veto or convince Congress to compromise on Clean Air, there's competitiveness involved and a certain determination to try to win. With something like Panama there's obviously that same tension and anxiety, and then after the operation a great sense of relief . . . but I'm not sure how I'd compare that to sports or a game. It's too serious. Lives are at stake. The emotions from sport are different. I'm not in that league in sport where my livelihood depends on it. So

sports are a relaxation for me, the competition, the camaraderie. Playing horseshoes with my sons is as much fun
as anything I do in life. Pure relaxation."

"A lot of people say that an important element in
sports is learning how to lose," I said.

"I'm a traditionalist. There is something about holding
your hand out to the victor that is proper, and I'm not
necessarily talking about white-flannel etiquette. It's certainly so in politics. The guy who walks off the field
whipped and is a poor loser lives with that and sometimes
in counterproductive ways . . . people remember: you
were such a bad sport in the primaries that you cost the
victor the final election because of the way you behaved.
So there's a clear analogy to sports."

"What about business?" I asked.

"I've been out of it for so long," the president said.

"The leveraged buyouts, the takeovers . . . "

"Much of it is offensive to me," he said. "The rich do
this just to get richer. It's become a game to some degree,
but it's not particularly pretty or attractive. Maybe I've
been in government too long, but I see some of the golden
parachutes, the golden handshakes—thank you very
much, a gold watch, and $30 million—and then I com-
pare this to public servants, who dedicate their lives to
government, and I think there's a disconnect here."

The two Bush boys rode past the office window on
their blue bicycles. They dropped in, the dogs at their
heels.

"Down, Ranger!" the president said.

"Do you think regulation might be a solution?" I
asked.

The president leaned back. "They're free to do it, and
I'm not going to propose legislation to do anything about

it because I believe in the freest possible market. But that doesn't mean I can adjust either to enormous debt or the magnitude of personal compensation that goes on these days."

"You can't just make it a question of conscience."

"Conscience is such a subjective quality," he replied. "Two honest people can differ on how something should be done. Fundamentals should be the guiding principle— doing the right things, upholding the values shaped by family. That's why I worry so about the dissolution of the family, the disadvantage that a kid starts off with if he or she doesn't enjoy a normal family life, a mother to read to him, and so forth."

"How does sport enter into this?" I asked.

"I don't think sport can be overemphasized. Fitness, of course. But it keeps telling you to go back to fundamentals—keep your head down, left arm straight, keep your eyes open, swing when you shoot, don't move your head . . . hundreds of basic rules. And on a less practical but highly important level, sports gives us its heroes—people who in some instances dispense that X Factor we've been talking about. I gauge people in sport not so much by performance but by sportsmanship. I tell people that my favorite sports hero is Lou Gehrig. He stayed in there; he was good (batted above .300 for years), and he played every game; he provided a certain sense of strength and stability and leadership to the team. I gather he was a very decent man, and when he left there wasn't a dry eye in Yankee Stadium because of the respect for his character as well as his ability."

The president looked at his watch and said it was just about time for the church service. Then it would be on to the day's sports activities.

These started with skeet shooting. The range was manned by marines in camouflage gear. The president had been given a new shotgun, a 20-gauge Weatherby. He was very proud of it. He showed us the silver inlay work on the breech—a beautiful design of a covey of quail. Just above the safety was an inlay of a horseshoe stake ringed by a horseshoe. "They thought of everything I like," he said. "But then look at this." He brought the gun up so I could read what was inscribed in barely visible letters on the barrel: MADE IN JAPAN. He shook his head. "The rest of it, the stock and so forth, was all made here," he said defensively.

He was pleased with his shooting. He had become adept at it during the war, shooting clay pigeons off the stern of his aircraft carrier. Twice as good as the rest of us—his brother Jonathan, his two nephews, and me—he led us quickly from one shooting station to the next, almost as if there were an internal rhythm that had to be applied. His targets disintegrated in fine black puffs of residual dust. We moved too slowly for him, fumbling with safety catches, dropping shells, ignoble on the doubles, and watching the pigeons float quietly to the grass untouched.

Next, tennis. We drove up to the courts in our carts. I suggested that the president play with my son, since I knew Taylor would want to tell his grandchildren one day that he had been partnered with the president. My partner was Lloyd Hatcher, slim and fast, and who had played briefly on the Virginia Slims circuit. The level of play was high and exciting. Taylor tumbled to the court à la Becker and made spectacular retrieves. The president was agile, especially at net, and they combined well as a team. The president kept up a spirited chatter. A badly missed shot involved "a high humiliation factor." An overzealous angle was referred to as the result of "a high arrogance factor." Once I heard him call out after he had hit a strong shot between us, "Hey, threading the needle . . . the X Factor!"

They were ahead in the first set 5–3, but we caught up and won in the tiebreaker. "How about another?"

It was chilly. A wind sighed through the pines. Beyond the fences, three Secret Service men with backs to the play stood looking out into the woods to check on anything moving out there. They could have been taken for bird-watchers, bored with tennis, and on the watch for a red-eyed vireo fluttering in the undergrowth. Beside them were valise-like bags that contained, I was told, Uzi automatic weapons. A phone at courtside suddenly rang.

The president was serving; his second ball was in the air. He was obviously startled—the familiar indoor sound of a telephone so odd to hear emerging from amid the trees. His serve went out by a foot. He strode across the court to pick up the receiver. We watched him, wondering what sort of news was so demanding as to interrupt a tennis game on his weekend. He bent over as if to hear better and then straightened up. He looked over at me. "It's for you!" he called out. He held out the receiver.

Oh, my God, I thought as I hurried toward him. *It's Buterakos, the Big Man! He's at the Camp David gate with a high school band and the Percheron! He's demanding entrance.*

Thankfully, it was not the Big Man, but a friend trying to get a message to me about a dinner party that night in New York; to his astonishment, he had been put through to the tennis courts. He recognized the president's voice. "My God," he said to a friend with him. "I think I've just been speaking to the president of the United States."

We played better in the second set. Perhaps the phone call had a slight psychological effect. Lloyd Hatcher got her game going—possibly because she didn't like the idea of being beaten by a thirteen-year-old, even if his partner was the president of the United States.

The president and I left by golf cart for the horseshoe court, leaving a contingent playing tennis. I told the president I had forgotten my cowboy hat. He grinned and said that he wouldn't bother going back to the house to fetch his; we'd play even.

The horseshoe facility is very fancy. It has a board with round pegs that are moved along a bar to keep track of the score. At both ends a bucket of water hangs from a crossbar, with a towel alongside to wipe off the shoes. The pits at either end are filled with the puttylike all-weather substance the president had described in his letter. The horseshoe slaps into it with the sound of a wet towel being dropped on the tiles of a bathroom floor. Rather than burrowing into soft surfaces such as sawdust or Georgia clay, a shoe that lands on its side tends to be rejected as if the surface were made of rubber; it leaps wildly out of the pit. I discovered this to my dismay during our warm-up tosses.

A Secret Service man took up his position by the scoring board to move the pegs. The match began. Across the macadam path, four-year-old Marshall moved among the paraphernalia of a little playground. Her mother was with her. Occasionally Marshall called across to her grandfather.

The first game did not go well at all. Playing to 21 points, the president jumped out to a 7–0 lead. I landed a ringer on one of his, which doubled my score to 6 points.

This was the last time I scored in that game. The man from the Secret Service moved the president's peg inexorably along the board. My peg remained permanently stuck at 6, as if fixed by glue. The president played very quickly, much as he had on the skeet range. Almost as soon as the last horseshoe of the set lofted toward the opposite stake, he was striding down the court. On more than one occasion one of my shoes struck the wooden border of the pit with a harsh clang and set off down the macadam walkway like a hoop hit with a stick.

The president won the second game 21–1. As we played, through my mind flitted a number of images and impressions—a mishmash of what had been suggested over the months by my advisers: focus, concentration, confidence, even snippets of athletic catchphrases not at all pertinent to horseshoes ("keep your eye on the ball," "never up, never in"). A curious background humming in my ears may well have been Dr. Tuthill's babbling brook.

Across the macadam path Marshall called out from her swing. "Hey, look how high!"

"Very high," the president said, looking over and smiling appreciatively.

The third game began. The man from the Secret Service started moving the president's peg. His granddaughter hopped off her swing and came over to have her coat unbuttoned. The president bent over and slipped a thong off a wooden button. He straightened and threw three ringers in a row. "Hey!" he called out.

"I see you've changed your pitching style, sir," I said. "Throwing the shoe laterally rather than how you did it the last time we played"—a professional appraisal which must have seemed utterly presumptuous coming from someone who had scored only 1 point in the last ten minutes.

"A little power outage there," the president said politely as one of my horseshoes bounced in front of the pit.

I remembered Billie Jean King's advice, one of her buzzwords—exaggerate, slow everything down—so I dawdled. I tried to block everything from my mind. My Zen friend's submarine appeared. I could sense the president's impatience as he stood alongside. I threw the horseshoe. It hit on its edge and bounded angrily toward the scorekeeper, who stepped aside to get out of its way.

The president took his turn. "Nice shot," I said. "Lovely."

The president's last shot was a perfect ringer. I had not scored a point since the middle of the second game. A debacle! I avoided the eyes of the gentleman from the Secret Service who had been moving our pegs, or more accurately, the president's. I hoped the president wasn't going to cry out "Vic Damone!" He didn't.

We got in the cart and headed up for lunch. "Not my day," I said. I wondered what the president was going to say to make me feel better about what had happened.

"I won't say anything at lunch about the horseshoes," he said with a big smile, "if you don't mention what happened at tennis."

The games weren't over. Just before lunch Jonathan Bush suggested a quick game of a Bush family favorite—tiddlywinks. The president agreed instantly—with no sense that he was being asked to indulge in a game that could hardly be called . . . well, *presidential*. He oversaw setting everything up. The table had to be the right height. The stewards hastened through the room. A blanket was produced and spread over the table. Various glasses and cups into which to chip the little disks, or winks, were brought in by the stewards and discarded as being too tall or too shallow. "John, do they play this game in the Philippines?" he asked. A steward shook his head. "A shame," the president said. "My mother is the great champion of the family."

The president picked me as his partner, perhaps reckoning that yet another loss at his hands might be too much for me, that I would crack under the humiliation and ride off into the forest on one of the blue bicycles. Taylor was partnered with Jonathan Bush.

We lost. The president stared at the table. "A rematch!" he called out. "Have to have a rematch."

"We'll hold up lunch," Mrs. Bush said to the head steward. This was said with no suggestion of impatience or resignation, but simply in the sense that something far more important had come up than sitting down to a luncheon table.

In the second game the president and I surged into the lead, but then we faltered. I chipped a disk far over the cup, off the table, and into his lap. "It's a knack," the president said as he put the disk back. "My mother could run off a string of six, seven. Just automatic from anywhere on the table."

We lost when Jonathan Bush chipped three disks into the cup.

"Not my day," I said to the president. "I let you down." After lunch I asked Jonathan Bush if there were any more family games scheduled. The helicopters were heading back to Washington at three o'clock—time enough to squeeze in a few more, it had occurred to me with some dismay.

He grinned and said in their boyhood when it rained at home in Greenwich there was inevitably an indoor golf tournament—putting through the house. "And, of course, knee football," he went on. "Tackle football except you move around on your knees."

"Very noisy," I suggested.

"A lot of thumping, yes. Lamps going over. We played in the front hall. Our brother, Bunky, weighed 280 pounds when he was at Hotchkiss School. Huge thighs. Very hard to bring down. Fay Vincent, who's gone on to become the commissioner of baseball, came over from next door when it rained. When he was a schoolboy he weighed about 250. Then they had a huge friend whose name I've forgotten who came over too. So right there you had almost a half-ton moving around on the floor of the front hall."

I looked around the living room and tried to imagine the stewards pushing the furniture back for knee football. I said I was awfully glad the sun had come out that morning at Camp David and that this had precluded rainy day sports.

■ ■ ■

ON THE FLIGHT back to New York, I asked Taylor what he would remember most about his weekend with the president.

He thought for a while. "I'll remember him hitting Mrs. Bush in the head with the tennis ball. I'll remember how he came and knocked on the door of our guest house and came in that first time with his cowboy hat, and how he made us feel at home. After that he never seemed like the president but just a very nice person, about the nicest person I ever met. Then just before he got on the helicopter to go back to Washington, I looked and he was wearing a brown suit and a red tie, and he was the president again. Just amazing!" He paused for a moment and then he said, "It was the best time I ever had in my life."

I wondered vaguely if he had been turned from an Independent into a Republican.

"What about you, Dad?" he asked.

"My bones ache," I told him. "I've never gone through anything quite like wallyball. I'll remember the stewards rushing around trying to find the proper-sized cup for tiddlywinks and a blanket for the table. I'll remember how badly I played at horseshoes and how well you played as the president's partner."

"I served a double-fault when we were ahead 5–3 in the first set. The pressure . . . "

"Doesn't compare to my collapse at horseshoes," I assured him. "One point in two games."

"Did you talk about the X Factor?" he asked.

"For a while," I said. "For him it seemed a lively combination of things—sportsmanship, confidence, concentration, fundamentals, adrenaline, maturity, trying your best always . . . and perhaps the most interesting thing he said was that in his case he had learned to perform better *because* of the public gaze rather than in spite of it."

I told Taylor that I had been reminded of what had been said about the prizefighter Muhammad Ali: that he needed the roar of the crowd to sustain him, much as Antaeus needed to touch the ground to support his strength; a journeyman fighter could beat Ali if they fought in a telephone booth.

"I should have come down to watch you play horseshoes," Taylor said. "It might have helped."

I sighed and said it wouldn't have made any difference

if he'd brought down the entire population of Maryland.

"He had his X Factor working for him," I said. "Mine didn't seem to be anywhere in sight."

After a moment he asked, "What does 'effigy' mean?"

"Well, it's a kind of dummy people make," I said, "usually of straw and old clothes, of someone they don't like. Then they hang it from a tree with a rope around its neck or burn it. It's a rather excessive way of letting off steam."

Taylor was looking out the window.

"You're thinking of the president's remark about Yale?"

"Yes," he said. "I guess they didn't get to know him, those people." He was still looking out the window. I could see the skyline of New York beyond.

I was glad he'd come. He'd exemplified a bit of the X Factor himself—flying around the tennis court, winning with the president at wallyball, and beating him at tiddlywinks: a far better record than mine.

As for me, a curious axiom of John Madden's came to mind. I had heard the former Oakland Raiders coach and now television commentator pronounce it at some point. It was: "Don't worry about the horse being blind. Load up the wagon." Madden added that he never had known quite what it meant, but it *sounded* pretty good. I think I have the gist of it, though. It seems appropriate enough. . . .

11

WHATEVER OUR OWN sense of him, President Bush couldn't win over the electorate in 1992. At the time, I wondered how an adversity of such magnitude would affect someone as competitive. In the summer of 1993 I wrote and asked if I could come to Houston and talk to him about this. If it worked out, I suggested I could use the material as a kind of coda for a future edition of *The X Factor*. I was quite prepared to be turned down. There had been hardly a word about him in the newspapers since the election. Obviously he was keeping to a low profile. To my surprise, he wrote back and said he'd be delighted to see me. But there were conditions. No discussion of politics. Absolutely none. Indeed, just before I left for Houston for my appointment with him, his secretary called to remind me of this.

We were to meet in his offices which are in a high-rise office building on Memorial Drive—a very modern edifice, a lobby with spotted marble, a glass atrium, and a large waterfall fountain. I took the elevator up to the ninth floor. In the president's outer office, I was told he was taping a tribute to Ted Williams, the baseball star. A retired volunteer, Jack Steel, appeared and offered to show me some of the items stored in various office rooms and awaiting the completion of the Bush museum on the grounds of Texas A&M. The most impressive of these was a large structure called "The Gate of Kuwait," which took up most of an empty room. Given to the president during his visit there in the spring of 1993, it stands well over six feet. A series of gold plaques listing the names of U.S. servicemen lost in the Gulf War outline a small door which is over a hundred years old. The door, apparently, symbolizes an old Kuwaiti proverb: "When a man gives you the key to his house, it means that you are the best and most valuable friend to him; when a man gives you the door of his house, it means that you are one of his family."

As we were inspecting the door, a secretary appeared and announced that the president was ready to see me.

His office is in a large room in the corner of the building. Almost immediately Mr. Bush shepherded me outside on a wide balustrade to show off the view—the clustered towers of downtown Houston, rising in the distance, shimmering slightly in the heat. I looked around for signs of a horseshoe pit—a length of Astroturf would have fit nicely where we were standing. Nothing. But as the president steered me back inside, I noticed a mahogany carrying case for horseshoes by the door, along with a fly rod tube.

He gave me a quick walkaround through the office itself—among the items on the walls a framed portrait of

Martin Van Buren, the first vice-president to be elected president, the map that Gorbachev gave Bush I remembered from Camp David, though no sign of the bullet-pocked target from Noriega's office. Or the knives. A Remington bronze of horses rested on a table, and on another, a photograph of the five living presidents taken during their appearance at the signing of NAFTA in Washington. A framed photograph of his dog, Ranger. In a bookcase I noted a volume of Izaak Walton's *The Compleat Angler,* a chunk of the Berlin Wall, and a bronze replica of Abraham Lincoln's hand. When the president remarked on the size of the latter, I remembered that in doing the research for the *Sports Illustrated* piece I had come across the fact that Lincoln could hold an axe out at arm's length from that hand for minutes at a time as a kind of parlor trick.

"Is that so?" the president said.

We sat down at either end of a low coffee table on which rested a large volume entitled *Men and Whales.* The president stretched out his legs. He was wearing a cowboy-style belt buckle.

"So . . . "

"Well, you're very good to see me, sir," I said.

"I've really gotten out of the interview business, politics and all that stuff," he said, "and I'm just not doing it. I'm very happy *not* to do it."

He went on to say that Leslie Stahl and Barbara Walters had both been after him, using the argument that his yearlong moratorium on interviews was coming to an end, each pining to have the first interview with him.

"I might extend the moratorium for a year," he said with a smile. "I don't have any inclination to get back into the crossfire. I'm doing some public speaking—that's the way I stay alive, pay the rent. My only political interest is in my two sons because both of them are going to be running for governor, George here in Texas, and Jeb in Florida. I can't believe it after the pounding we took last year, but they're going to do it, so there we are."

"You'll be back in the fray again," I said.

"Well, I hope to help them. But you've got to figure whether it's good or bad for me to help when they should be going after it on their own merits where they both have darn good records."

I shuffled my papers and said I was duty-bound not to ask him any political questions, not even about his sons.

"Fair enough."

"So what did you do after the election?" I asked.

"In Maine I just sat there and watched the tide come in and go out. That was important. I'm trying hard to be a nonimperial ex-president. It's a very pleasant, private life out here, but it wasn't easy at first."

"What do you miss most, if anything?"

"The decision-making, the actual involvement, and trying to make things happen," he said. "I liked that. I liked a lot of it. When it's gone, it takes a while to get over it. So that was hard. You sit there and there are no decisions; nothing to sign; nobody wants to know what you think on this, or that. It was just a cold turkey shift; but it is fine and it's the way it should be."

"What about politics," I asked. "I don't mean anything specific," I added nervously. "Just in general."

"I don't miss the politics of it at all, dealing with an adversarial Senate and all that," he said. "When I went back to Washington for the Rabin-Arafat meeting I saw those guys up there and they looked very nice and very pleasant. I'd rather have it that way than to be back in the mix . . ."

"And the press?" I asked

"I'm not interested in getting back into that business at all," he said with a shake of his head. "Last year was not a pleasant year. There's an unaccountability in the press that worries me very much . . . assigning motives that you know they've got wrong. But you can't do anything about it. And it's not just national, it's international. My friends who are leaders in Europe tell me the same thing. So I can confidently tell you I don't miss that at all."

"And the loss?"

"I don't have as much regret as I thought I would have. I have no bitterness at all, I must say."

"How do you get through something like that?" I asked.

"Family," he said. He leaned back in his chair. "And besides," he went on, "I don't think we ever got caught up in what we lost so much that we felt that we deserved it or that it was part of our being. Though we were in Washington for twelve years, we were always able to keep a reasonably good perspective. So it wasn't hard in terms of perks and all that. Afterwards, we climbed on as tourists at Continental Airline, and though it was quite a change from Air Force One, and the majesty of it, it was fine. When we got back to Houston, Barbara walked into the kitchen, cooked the meal, I did the dishes, and it didn't miss a beat."

"It's all right."

"It's all right. People are very accommodating and pleasant. It was nice to go to Fenway Park, sit there right on the field, watch the baseball and not get booed." He grinned. "That's the other side of it, of course. You don't have to carry around the political baggage.

"Humor helps a lot," he said suddenly.

I asked if he could give an example.

The president nodded and said that not long after the election his dog, Ranger, had died, which had been very hard for him to accept. "I didn't think that at my age anything could mean that much to me. But then I got a letter from a close friend named Fred Zeder. Zeder wrote in his letter: 'Dear George: I'm sorry to hear that Ranger went *paws up*.' I thought that was a slightly insensitive way of putting it," the president said with a grin, "but it suddenly got me into a better frame of mind about my poor Ranger."

"Paws up."

"That's right. Without humor we'd be dead. My kids tease me about being unemployed. On my passport I put down my status as 'retired.' Barbara has put down as hers: 'home-maker.' "

I asked what the two of them had done immediately after the election.

"Well, we went on a trip. I took Barbara on one of those Love Boat cruise-liners—the Regal Princess, something like that. You talk about a laugh, that was fun. Everywhere we went on the ship, people came up to us. Barbara said, 'Hey, listen, if *half* the people on this boat who told you they voted for you did so, you wouldn't be here on the Love Boat.' They gave us the warmest reception. One time I came out of the sauna totally naked and some guy suddenly appeared and said, 'Mind if I take your picture?' I said, 'Hell, yes, I mind if you take my picture—do you mind waiting.' And Barbara, same thing when she was coming out of the hairdresser. The captain, a wonderful fellow, saw that people in just the friendliest way were overwhelming us and he took us up to his flying bridge to give us some peace. We sat up there like it was our own yacht. He had a man and the whole thing over his arm . . ."

"A napkin," I suggested.

"A napkin. 'What will you have, sir?' he asked, and the caviar was forthcoming and it was heaven. A beautiful boat actually. Glass chandeliers. Statues. Grassroots, marvelous tourist thing. One of the Princesses. It was such fun."

I asked if it had been easy to persuade his wife to go on a Love Boat cruise.

"She didn't know. A surprise. She thought I'd lost it. But now back here in Houston, we're getting to do more practical things. Building a house. That's helped. Barbara's like a new bride. For forty-nine years we've never built a house from scratch."

I said that I'd heard the house was being constructed on a surprisingly narrow plot of land.

The president nodded and said that he had been ridiculed for that. "Don't you remember? The L.A. Times had a cartoon suggesting the only way that an elitist like me could build on this narrow lot would be to have a cantilevered structure sticking out over my neighbors' houses! The Democrats sent some of their more flamboyant members out there to the lot and held a press conference. 'Look at this. He says this is where he's going to live. It's ridiculous.' "

"They didn't believe it."

"Absolutely not. In fact not only did they not believe it, but used it as a rather nasty way of saying, 'Well, the guy's lying about what he's planning to do in the future.' "

"What *about* the future?"

"Well, we're both working on books. I can say that without any problem." He went on to say with considerable pride that Barbara's was a "big" book. By comparison, he was rather self-deprecatory about his own memoir—one that he is working on with his former security adviser, Brent Scowcroft. "It will be dusted off every few years by the Foreign Policy Association wonks. Actually, I think it will be a good book. It will tell how decisions were made on German reunification, NAFTA, China, and Desert Storm."

I asked how the collaboration worked.

The president explained that it was not going to be an "As Told To" or "George Bush with Brent Scowcroft" but rather that the two would function as a pair.

"Would you write one chapter, and then Scowcroft the next?"

"Well, no. He's got the pen, writing away, and then I will come in and work on it from actual notes out of my diaries. We haven't quite sorted out how to do it. Of course, the publisher will want people getting mad at each other, stuff like that. Anecdotes."

I asked if he could give an example of the latter.

He leaned back in his chair and began a little story about Mrs. Gorbachev at a dinner at the Russian Embassy when he was the vice-president. After a long meal the Russians had produced entertainment in the form of a very large opera singer.

"She was enormous, not a particularly attractive woman," the president said, "but of course with a beautiful voice. After a while—actually it was about midnight; we should have been out of there an hour before—I turned to Mrs. Gorbachev and kiddingly said, 'Oh, this is lovely music. I think I'm falling in love.' Mrs. Gorbachev looked over and very seriously she whispered, 'You better not. Remember Gary Hart!' "

"She was being serious?"

"Oh absolutely. Not a smile on her face."

At this point—just in case I took this to be a derogatory story about Hart—he mentioned that he'd met the former presidential aspirant and liked him. "A very pleasant fellow." He'd heard that Hart was doing a lot of business with the Russians.

We got talking about fishing—which he had done since the election off Labrador, Florida, and in the Bahamas. In the Bahamas he and Nick Brady, the former secretary of the Treasury, had caught eight bonefish in one day's fishing, one of them a ten-pounder. ("Just heaven!") That day on the flats they had spotted a permit, one of the great game fish of the Caribbean. "We didn't have the right bait for permit—crab rather than shrimp," the president was saying. "But the guide said to cast just beyond a ray that was lying there flat on the sand bottom. I never thought I could, but I threw it and it kind of slid past the ray's back right down in front of this permit's nose. He ducked at it twice and then just lazily swam away."

"A shame," I said.

The president said if the permit had been hooked, the guide would have started up the motor to chase after the fish to keep him from breaking the line. "Probably couldn't have done it in time. I asked the guide, 'How big a fish was that?' and he said, 'Thirty pounds.' A gigantic thing."

I asked what other sports activities he was up to. He said he had stopped his jogging because of a bad hip which didn't hurt when he was running but did at night, and the doctors had said, "Listen, you better stop."

"So I fast-walk, and I do that a fair amount, and golf, of course, which is not great exercise, particularly if you're running around in a golf cart."

I was reminded that Bush was noted on the Arundel Golf Course at Kennebunkport for speeding around the course—the elapsed time almost as important as the score. The president brightened and said they had set a good record that summer—he and the club pro, Ken Raynor, had done 18 holes in one hour and twenty-four minutes, holing out everything. "And we weren't even trying," he added.

"Do you work as hard in Maine as you do here?"

"No. We've got our grandkids and a tiny little outboard and I love watching that, yelling at them. Maine is a different tempo. There's a feeling of predictability and steadiness to Maine that we love. My mother was born there. Our kids come there to home. It's their anchor. It's a stable, a glorious base for us. We've had a lot of tennis there. Chris Evert came to Kennebunkport with her husband, Andy Mills, skiing champion, wonderful athlete, great competitor. We got right out and played—my son, Marvin, who's a fine player, and Andy Mills playing Chrissie and me. I think we split sets. It was fun. She's a terrific competitor, even in a little match hacking around: 'Bend the knees. Go for it! Get it, you can get it!'

"The thing that got me a little was the next day. I saw Marvin and a couple of other guys getting ready, and Chris all suited up in her tennis garb, and I said, 'What's the match? How are we going to do this?'

" 'Dad, we hadn't counted on you playing.'

"I realized at that moment that I had been unceremoniously dumped. The only consolation was that Andy Mills had also been dumped. Neither of us measured up to what Marvin considered the Walker Point standard. We went down and watched and needled them about it."

I asked if he enjoyed playing in the celebrity tournaments that seemed to attract so many from the political as well as the entertainment world.

"I don't like those celebrity events. Ever since I hit a guy on the ass with a Titleist off a seven-wood shot in the Doug Sanders Tournament, I've been gun-shy about these events."

I asked: "Did the guy you hit on the ass with a Titleist complain or sue?"

The president mused about what had happened. "I was looking down this funnel of spectators," he said. "An unforgiving funnel. I told them, 'Please step back. I'm not a good golfer.' And they moved an inch. Actually, this was my *second* shot, my tee shot having zoomed over their heads. I'd've thought they'd have headed for the hills. But they didn't. They moved back an inch. So I took this seven-wood—Calloway seven—and *hooked* the shot for some reason. I usually slice. And zap! I could literally hear the ball hitting this guy. I rushed up. He was smiling. I said, 'Oh, my gosh, I feel so badly.' He was holding a baby in his arms! But it wasn't the baby I'd hit, thank goodness; it was him. So I sent him a Care package—some presidential golf balls left over and a couple of things. I got back the nicest letter: 'I'm a longtime supporter. Nothing gave me more pleasure than seeing you out there.' "

■ ■ ■

WE NEVER DID get to play a third game of horseshoes. The president had appointments that afternoon. He invited me to join him and his wife to see a baseball game that evening—the Astros against the Giants. We sat in a box at field level. Sure enough, no boos. Fans applauded as he came down the aisle to our seats. Mrs. Bush kept score. She had watched her husband playing for Yale in his undergraduate days and, as she put it, had become "rapidly fluent in baseball."

I remembered that a couple of Bush's teammates had gone into the majors. I asked if he'd had the opportunity.

"Well, one day I went 3 for 5 in a game against North Carolina State and the scouts came rushing up to Ethan Allen, who was the coach. 'Hey, who is this kid?' Then they looked at my averages and went away in a hurry. That was my problem—batting. I batted seven or eight in the order. I used to joke that I played 'second cleanup.' Still, baseball has always been a great love. When I was a kid we followed the game very closely. Read the sports pages. I was a big Red Sox fan—Jimmie Foxx, Bobby Doerr. I could recite the batting averages of the top twenty hitters in both leagues. Lou Gehrig was a childhood hero. Caught a foul ball in Yankee Stadium. I loved *all* that."

People dropped by. Very friendly atmosphere. Hard to concentrate on the game. A message appeared on the scoreboard: *Lisa will you marry me?* A ball bounced just over the fingertips of the Astros pitcher. Groans from the Bushes. Someone behind me said "Luck." Someone else remembered that Branch Rickey had once said, rather solemnly, that "luck was the residue of design." I wrote it down on my baseball scorecard, deciphering it the other day. I have no idea who said it. The president? A friend dropped by the box and handed the president a cap that bore the message "Stop Whining!" which seemed a curious if not questionable gift. The president did not substitute it for the baseball cap he was wearing, though he profusely thanked the person who had given it to him. "Just great to have this!" He looked back at the field. He stretched out his legs. The Giants pitcher came out of the dugout on the way to the mound. The fans began to clap for an Astros rally. "Heaven!" the president said.